PRAISE FOR *WHAT MAI*

"The Assessments 24x7 team has written a must-read primer for anyone who is looking to optimize their human capital investments…Read this book—and learn from one of the best."

Lisa Patrick, *Forbes* and *Entrepreneur* contributor, business development strategist, influencer

"I was first trained on Behavior Profiling Systems almost forty years ago. Today, one thing I know to be true is that Dr. Tony Alessandra is the world's leading expert in this field. Tony, along with Brandon Parker, and Jennifer Larsen, has taken their many years of combined experience and compiled one of the most comprehensive books I've yet to see on this topic. I recommend it without hesitation."

Dr. Ivan Misner, *NY Times* bestselling author and founder of BNI

"As a global firm leader in my franchise, ActionCOACH, *What Makes Humans Tick?* is a transformational textbook on developing people to be the best version of themselves."

Barb Kyes, managing partner, ActionCOACH Tampa Bay, 2020 Global Assessment award winner

"The authors of *What Makes Humans Tick?* have nailed the answer to the question! This treatise is a must-read for anyone truly attempting to master our challenges of the people business. It will enhance your understanding of human behavior and give you useful tips for strategizing with others."

Don Hutson, co-author of the *NYTimes, Wall Street Journal* #1 best-Seller, *The One Minute Entrepreneur*, and CEO of U. S. Learning

"What I love most about [this] book is that reading it is like having a truly fascinating conversation with an expert on people. You will learn so much in these pages and it will feel effortless, due to the way [it] explains important concepts in an easy to understand and apply way. This book will have a real impact on your connection with others and the results you get."

Liz Masen, CEO, Athlete Assessments

"If there is a Holy Grail in the science of human behavior, *What Makes Humans Tick?* is it! This book is a must read for everyone in leadership! Your quest to improve the performance of your people should begin with understanding them through the use of scientifically validated assessments. But a single assessment is not adequate enough to understand the "whole person." If you want to reduce your costs and maximize the ROI in your largest investment—your human capital—read this book!"

Kevin McCarthy, CEO, BlindSpots Leadership Development, and author
BlindSpots: Why Good People Make Bad Choices

"Delivering the message of 'The Platinum Rule' been the game-changer in my workshops and transforming dysfunctional relationships in my clients' businesses. Ever since I have discovered the key learnings from this book and practice it on a daily basis, not only have my own relationships changed, I have been able to help thousands of people to communicate more effectively and it's so simple."

Jaymini Mistry, director, Think Space Co.

"This fast-moving, enjoyable book shows you how to unlock your full potential for success and high-performance living."

Brian Tracy, best-selling author and Hall-of-Fame speaker

"Tests, Exams, X-rays, MRIs, Lipid Panels, Turn-your-head-and-cough, and many other tools gather data for physical health awareness. But to determine the facts and strategies for human capital awareness and success in professional, personal, and social relationships, including career satisfaction and employer fulfilment, this is the book to help understand the tools in the science of people's styles…their strengths and potential. Reading this book will teach you what you need to know about assessments. You will learn the right combination of the best validated assessments for understanding the whole person to identify *What Makes Humans Tick?*."

Jane Roqueplot, career advancement coach, résumé writer, and behavioral analyst

"When I learned we had the opportunity to provide coach graduates with a dashboard so they can give many different assessments, my response was, "that is exactly what I have been looking for—sign us up!" Now, in this book, Dr. Tony Alessandra, Brandon Parker, and Jennifer Larsen do a great job of laying out the value of a combined assessment package with insight on exactly what each measures, and a comprehensive explanation of how they work together. This book is ideal for coaches who currently use assessments or are considering the use of assessments."

Cathy Liska, MCC, CEO and founder of the Center for Coaching Certification, author in the Coaching Perspectives series

"*What Makes Humans Tick?* is so well-researched and provides a deep level of detail about various assessments all in one convenient volume. It is invaluable to coaches, leaders and anyone who wishes to go beyond the surface in these areas and learn how behavior, motivators, critical thinking and decision-making all play a role in the complex realm of understanding personality. I learned so much and highly recommend it!"

Ira Tau, Certified Executive Coach, Assessments 24x7 Advanced Certified Practitioner

"*What Makes Humans Tick?*" is the key to the lock on interacting, successfully working, effective communication, and leading people and organizations towards success. Your understanding and implementation of the guidance in this book will make the difference in the success or challenge(s) of your leadership. *"What Makes Humans Tick?"* is a must-read for all!"

Curtis E. Johnson, Jr. MBA, SHRM-CP, CEO The CUVEY Group, LLC

"If you are in business, you are in the people business. *What Makes Humans Tick?* gives you clarity and understanding of how to influence, relate to, and build deep long-lasting relationships by understanding who a person truly is. Communication is a big barrier to deepening relationships. The assessments, teachings, and recommendations in *What Makes Humans Tick?* will help you be the best communicator you can be."

Monte Wyatt, CEO & Master Executive Coach, AddingZEROS, author of *Pulling Profits Out of a Hat*

"Learn how to improve and strengthen relationships across all levels of employees. A must read for anyone responsible for getting the most out of their employees."

Greg Carkhuff, CEO HRD Press, Inc.

"As a student of leadership and human potential, I am always excited to learn more about what makes people tick. Understanding this can help us lead and influence people on our teams, in our homes, and the world around us. Dr. Tony Alessandra is a brilliant teacher in the arena of the personalities and how others think, communicate, and work together as a team. If you are a leader of others and your role requires you to coach people to perform at a higher level of performance then I recommend you grab *What Makes Humans Tick?* today and learn all you can from Tony and his co-author's experience to take your team and your own leadership potential to the next level."

Mike Harbour, CEO of Harbour Resources

"I have worked with Dr. Tony and his team for 10 years and I have always found them to be honorable, competent, innovative and client focused. This latest book supports those findings. It is scientific, people-centric, and easy to assimilate. You would be well served to include this in your human performance library."

Greg Smith, The Maui Analysis Group and creator of the Executive Summary reports

"Working as an ICF MCC Performance coach awareness in the coaching process is key for our clients. The book *What Makes Human Tick?* is an extraordinary explanation of how to have and create more awareness. In my coaching process one or more evidence based coaching assessments are key to explore together with the client's outcomes, reflection and distinctions. All this is beautifully written in the book. Highly recommend!"

Roel C. Schaart, ICF MCC, MCP Disc & Motivators, Advanced Certified Practitioner 123 Assessments

"As a professional speaker and business consultant, I use profiling tools a lot in my business, working with clients to bring out their best. I found *What Makes Humans Tick?* a great read and I'm now recommending it to my clients as it shows them how to unlock the potential of their people. This book is ideal for coaches, consultants, managers and leaders everywhere."
Lindsay Adams OAM CSP, CEO, Teamocracy & author of *The DNA of Business Relationships*

"*What Makes Humans Tick?* encompasses all of the key advances in psychometrics assessment tools and integrates them to provide a comprehensive and deeper understanding of an individual's strengths and opportunities. It's a powerful tool in an ever-competitive world where leadership development is critical."
George A. Metanias, CEO Elevate LLC

"*What Makes Humans Tick?* is a reference to better understand what is being measured through the assessments and how best to interpret them. A real goldmine, full of concrete examples to better understand human nature, to be put in the hands of every coach, consultant and HR manager, even the most expert in the field."
Eric Grossberger, Coach and leadership trainer at Erudia France

"It was great to read it and to see all the assessments discussed together in one book. The authors of *What Makes Humans Tick?* have done a great job with so much valuable information about multiple ways of understanding people explained very well and also a lot of information on how to adapted this knowledge in your day-to-day life situations. This is a must read for everyone who is working with other people."
Johan Trommelen, Assessments 24x7 Netherlands Master Distributor & DISC and Motivators specialist

"Finally, there is a guide that takes the mystery out of people assessments with step-by-step application tips to maximize results. Full of practical, real- world examples, this is a must-read for anyone who wants to improve their ability to effectively hire, manage and work with others."
Mike Esterday, CEO Integrity Solutions

"A masterpiece on understanding how people behave, think, and what drives them. Especially useful when considering hiring someone or helping us all get along better. By truly understanding who we are, recognizing the differences between us and, of course, following Tony's Platinum Rule… we will be building bridges instead of walls. This book will help you do just that! Educational, powerful and very well written."

Laura A Bruno ACP, CPBA, CPMA

"When you understand a person, it's amazing what you can accomplish. *What Makes Humans Tick?* is a valuable guide to understanding the human structure and its resources. It clearly shows how you can make it to the top together in communicating well, with the best for all. It offers clear and quick guidance on identifying and understanding those who think differently from you and improving your relationship with them."

Ursula Lork, Psychologist

WHAT MAKES HUMANS TICK?

DISC AND MOTIVATORS

EXPLORING THE BEST VALIDATED ASSESSMENTS

BRANDON PARKER

JENNIFER LARSEN, MAED, MSP, MBA

TONY ALESSANDRA, PHD

WITH MATTHEW DICKSON

INDIE BOOKS
INTERNATIONAL®

ISBN: 978-1-952233-35-7
Library of Congress Control Number: 2020922647

Dr. Tony Alessandra created The Platinum Rule®. The Platinum Rule® is a registered trademark of Dr. Anthony J. Alessandra.

Dorothy Downey created the original Personal Profile System® (PPS).

Personal Profile System® (PPS) is a registered trademark of Carlson Learning Company Corporation.

Designed by Joni McPherson, mcphersongraphics.com

INDIE BOOKS INTERNATIONAL, INC®
2424 VISTA WAY, SUITE 316
OCEANSIDE, CA 92054
www.indiebooksintl.com

CONTENTS

CHAPTER 1

Why People Prediction Is Risky Business

People prediction is risky business. So much is at stake, and there are so many variables involved in getting it right—including environment, situation, relationships, relevancies, knowledge, skills, experience, education, and more.

With these circumstances, do you trust your gut, or do you trust data? Many scientists are credited with the phrase, "In God we trust. All others must bring data."

Professor William Thompson (Lord Kelvin) was an eminent Irish-born physicist with a wide range of interests who lived from 1824 to 1907. Lord Kelvin studied the properties of heat, such as the correct value of absolute zero (-459.67 degrees Fahrenheit, to be precise), and absolute temperatures are stated in units of kelvin in his honor. He was knighted by Queen Victoria for his ingenuity in laying the transatlantic telegraph cable. Best remembered for his talent for theoretical mathematics and electricity, Lord Kelvin is credited with doing much to unify the emerging field of physics in its modern form.

The man believed in numbers and is famous for the following quotation:

> *When you can measure what you are speaking about, and express it in numbers, you know something about it. When you cannot express it in numbers, your knowledge is of a meager and unsatisfactory kind; it may be the beginning of knowledge, but you have scarcely, in your thoughts, advanced to the stage of science.*

The purpose of this book is to advance the science and understanding of people assessments. Today's modern assessments work by introducing scientific measurements to a variety of elements, including someone's critical thinking skills, motivations, potential skill proficiencies, work styles, behavioral characteristics, personal values, learning preferences, emotional awareness of self and others, and more.

Modern Online Assessments Reduce Risk And Leverage Human Capital

For much of the twentieth century, the science of assessments benefited only wealthy companies that could afford the costly investment. To be truly accurate, these assessments needed to be administered in person and the results calculated manually by PhDs. This made the science of assessments cost-prohibitive for the average company that lacked the resources of the Fortune 500. When it came to maximizing return on people investments with assessments, it was the classic case of the rich got richer.

In the twenty-first century, there came a leveling of the playing field through online assessments. Thanks in part to the digital revolution, manual assessments developed and reviewed by PhDs were replaced by modern computing power, algorithms, and system calculations. The evolution of online technology removed the cost barriers, so even the smallest business could benefit from the science of assessments.

Small and medium-sized businesses could now have access to what the big companies knew, that modern online assessments reduce risk and take the guesswork out of the greatest business variable of them all: human capital.

While the theory of human capital can be traced back to Adam Smith in the eighteenth century, much credit for the quest to understand the concept is given to a pair of Chicago economists: Theodore Schultz, a Nobel Prize winner in economics, and Gary Becker, who published the book *Human Capital* in 1964.

An organization is often said to only be as good as its people. Schultz and Becker, economics professors at the University of Chicago, believed human capital was like any other type of capital; it could be invested in to improve the quality and level of production. They believed managing human capital comes down to workforce acquisition, management, and optimization.

"The importance of human capital is now taken for granted," stated an article titled "The People's Champion" in the August 3, 2017 issue of *The Economist*. "What is more controversial is the question of how to cultivate it."

As any organization leader knows, the biggest cost of doing business is often human compensation. According to 2018 data from the U.S. Bureau of Labor Statistics, total employer compensation costs for private industry workers averaged $34.19 per hour worked. Total employer compensation costs for state and local government labor averaged $49.23 per hour worked.

"Typically, labor cost percentages average 20 to 35 percent of gross sales," stated business journalist William Adkins in a June 29, 2018 Houston Chronicle article. "A service business might have an employee percentage of 50 percent or more, but a manufacturer will usually need to keep the figure under 30 percent."

With the labor costs of doing business so high, it makes financial sense that an organization should invest in obtaining and optimizing its people.

> The best assessments optimize human capital investments by revealing core behavioral, motivational, emotional, and thinking styles, and seeking to create effectiveness and synergy using them.

The scientific advances in assessments are being noted by thought leaders and the media. The cover story of the June 22, 2015 *Time* magazine was about the use of assessments to predict and coach employee behavior. Author Eliza Gray devoted five pages to the main reasons why so many employers were turning to assessments. Gray commented that when big data is combined with analytics, outcomes for almost anything can be optimized—even people.

Some Say Talent Optimization Requires Art, Not Science

Some critics of assessments dismiss what they term "personality tests" as meaningless entertainment, a fad that won't die, or a distraction like astrology. "Personality" is more encompassing than just a single perspective of traits or descriptors and includes more than just behavioral analysis; it is so much more complex and involves things like character, emotions, and more. Additionally, assessment experts bristle at the media's use of the word "test" as shorthand; an assessment is not a test, because there are no right or wrong answers.

Here is a typical example of the criticism directed toward assessments. Critics like Oxford University English Professor Merve Emre are appalled that "one in five Fortune 1000 companies uses some means of personality testing to screen job candidates, both to hire the right type of person and to eliminate unfavorable types."[1]

Critics bring up valid concerns. Thousands of assessments are available, and the quality varies. Organizations can use the wrong assessments in the

---

[1] *Washington Post*, "Can You Type?", Sept. 10, 2018

wrong situations. Not all assessments are created equal, and some designed for a purpose like career development can be misapplied in the hiring process. Job applicants may manipulate the assessment by giving answers they think the employer wants to hear. Assessments can be biased. Some assessments have come under scrutiny by government regulators like the Equal Employment Opportunity Commission (EEOC).

Others argue that hiring and managing people is more art than science. Data is all well and good, these critics point out, but data should only go so far. Recruiting requires a leap of faith. Hiring executives are urged to trust their instincts, which ignores the possibility that many great potential hires are being eliminated based on things like unforeseen or underacknowledged biases.

Human judgment must always be part of the equation. But going with your gut, usually based on your first impressions of a person, is a gross miscalculation. Instincts cannot be measured, and your knowledge of the person may be limited and unsatisfactory.

Would you trust a doctor to make a prognosis without determining the proper diagnosis? If a doctor did not order tests before surgery, you would be seriously concerned. As the saying goes, prescription before diagnosis is malpractice.

What Doctor Would Not Use MRI Tests?

Think of quality assessments as MRI tests constructed to evaluate and reveal someone's complete cognitive makeup. Doctors know MRIs are well-validated, highly predictive assessments—and just as they need the judgment gained through experience to interpret the results correctly, any sophisticated people assessment tool needs educated and thorough interpretation as well.

In the *Harvard Business Review*, Whitney Martin summed up both the opportunity and the challenge:[2]

> *Personality tests are most effective when combined with other measures with higher predictive validity, such as integrity or cognitive ability. Using well-validated, highly predictive assessment tools can give business owners and managers a significant leg up when trying to select candidates who will become top producers for the organization. However, all assessment approaches are not created equal. And some will not offer a significant return on your investment.*

Like any investment, the human capital investment in assessments does not offer a guaranteed return. Martin cited a 2014 Aberdeen study that noted only 14 percent of organizations have data to prove the positive business aspects of their assessments. To select the tools that impact the bottom line requires a careful analysis of the most effective assessment for accomplishing specific objectives.

In other words, it is critical to use the right tool for the right job. To do otherwise is wasteful at best, and reckless at worst.

Reducing The Risk With Reliable Assessments

There once was a magazine cartoon that showed a father talking to his elementary-school-aged son. The father said, "I'm a social scientist, son. I can't explain electricity or stem cells, but if you want to know what makes human beings tick, I'm your guy."

The social science of using assessments to understand what makes humans tick, indeed for dozens of possible applications, continues to gain traction. One piece of evidence is marketplace popularity.

The marketplace is speaking about the increased reliability of online assessments. According to research by the Society for Human Resource Man-

---

[2] *HBR*, "The Problem with Using Personality Tests for Hiring," August 27, 2014

agement (SHRM), some experts estimate that as many as 60 percent of workers are now asked to take workplace assessments.

In 2015, Dori Meinert wrote in *HR Magazine* that based on the findings of a study completed by Human Capital Media, "The $500-million-dollar-a-year industry has grown about 10 percent annually in recent years. While many organizations use personality testing for career development, about 22 percent use it to evaluate job candidates."[3]

A big reason for the growth is the increased reliability of the assessments.

But the problem with the assessment industry is it is unregulated. There is no governing or accrediting body that certifies assessments for scientific validity and protects organizations from using assessments with adverse impacts.

That is why we began a quest to find the best validated and reliable instruments that would boost professional performance beyond anything previously available within the people analysis field by exploring the whole person. The right assessments would help develop more self-aware leaders, optimize high-performance teams, and select and retain top-producing employees.

We've Come A Long Way Since Myers-Briggs

An example of an assessment from the twentieth century that greatly advanced the field is the Myers-Briggs Type Indicator. This popular assessment deserves credit for offering an affordable way to analyze and discuss the differences of people in the workplace.

The science of assessments has greatly advanced since the advent of this personality type indicator. As one organizational psychologist critic put it, when it comes to accuracy, Myers-Briggs is better than a horoscope but less reliable than a heart monitor.

In her book, *The Personality Brokers: The Strange History of Myers-Briggs and the Birth of Personality Testing*, Merve Emre takes the assessment to

---

[3] *HR Magazine*, "What Do Personality Tests Really Reveal?", June 1, 2015

task, concluding it has no basis in real science—since those who answer its questions more than one time, often arrive at different type designations each time they are evaluated. Taken by over two million people each year, the Myers-Briggs Type Indicator is used by universities, several branches of the military, and, according to TheMyersBriggs.com, by more than 88 percent of the Fortune 500 companies. It is a curiosity to Emre why the test remains one of the world's most popular personality assessments.

However, this criticism misses the important place Myers-Briggs has in the history of assessments. Myers-Briggs was a voice in the wilderness in the 1900s that pointed the way to something better to come. A similar case could be made for the Analytical Engine created by British mathematician Charles Babbage in the 1800s, which led to today's modern computing power that makes online assessments possible. Both were rudimentary beginnings that have led to something truly powerful for businesses of any size.

Why So Many Have Switched To People Predictive Analytics

In the high-stakes world of human capital, it does not pay to bet on the wrong assessment.

As one executive put it, when hiring, he feels there is a fifty-fifty chance the person will work out; with the data from quality assessments, he feels he has improved the odds to a three out of four chance the new hire will succeed. This executive felt the less work experience the candidate has—like recent college graduates—the greater the importance of the assessment data.

Thousands of assessments, many available as online tools, are in use today to help organizations achieve desired outcomes for hiring and candidate selection, performance evaluations, skills training, team building, conflict management, promotion and succession planning, organizational restructuring, employee retention, and leadership development.

When it comes to understanding what makes top talent tick, it is possible to measure what you are speaking about and express it in numbers. The best assessments evaluate and reveal a person's cognitive makeup expressed in numerical values. It's been shown time and time again that having a knowledge of assessments can be used to reduce risks and create more effective relationships and outcomes.

No Silver-Bullet Assessment

Many people in the last century searched for the silver-bullet assessment. Of the thousands of assessments, where was the one best tool that could reveal everything necessary to know about a person? No single assessment was ever found.

The problem was the twentieth century's single assessment approach was overly simple; it ignored the complexity of the issue and of people. After decades of work and research within the assessment industry, Dr. Tony Alessandra, founder and chairman of Assessments 24x7, and coauthor of this book, sought a different approach to assessment-based solutions. His quest was to find a twenty-first-century, comprehensive methodology that could provide deeper insight in a simple, practical, and applicable way.

Alessandra observed that human beings are far too complex for a single assessment solution. He also noted that it did not work to string together a random assortment of assessments with no rhyme or reason. Multiple views were the key, but not just any views would do. Using a foundational mantra from the Higher Learning Commission, the accreditor for colleges and universities in the United States, Alessandra knew multiple measures would further provide a pattern of powerful evidence that would connect the dots to allow for congruency in understanding what makes someone tick.

His research led him to what this book will explore: each assessment measures a different, yet important, dimension of human behavior or cognition. Furthermore, each of the assessments is its own unique assessment instrument, offering a customized set of reports, validity studies, coaching materials, workshop materials, certification training, and more.

Assessments 24x7 has done significant work in not only structuring this assessment-based methodology as a packaged solution, but has sought diligently to overcome concerns and naysayers of assessments by providing scientifically-backed, validated, and reliable products and resources to ensure that these tools can be used with confidence to change lives. Countless clients, companies, and coaches have seen firsthand how assessments and proper interpretation can make a difference for individuals, personal and professional relationships, and organizations of varying size.

The next chapter examines the research that led to this innovative solution of comprehensive and foundational assessments, and provides more detail about each of these online tools.

APPLYING ASSESSMENT SCIENCE

After decades of work and research on how to assess the dimensions of people, Dr. Tony Alessandra and his team found these scientifically based assessments would provide the best foundational approach:

DISC: the world's number one behavioral profiling tool

Motivators: a measure of the Seven Universal Dimensions of Motivation that drive us all

Critical Thinking (based on the Hartman Value Profile): a measure of critical thinking and processing ability, decision-making skills, and situational bias

Emotional Intelligence: a measure of our EIQ to help users understand their own emotions and the way in which emotions impact interactions with others

Assessments Provide A Powerful Picture

To understand how assessments offer a powerful approach to understanding human beings, consider this fable.

This tale originated in India. The first written version is traceable to an ancient Buddhist text, written in the first century BCE. The story is probably older than that and teaches a universal truth:

A group of blind men heard that a strange animal, called an elephant, had been brought to the village, but none of them were aware of its shape and form. Out of curiosity, they agreed they must inspect and know it by touch. When they found the strange beast, they groped about it. In the case of the first person, whose hand landed on the trunk, he said: "This is like a thick snake." The blind man who placed his hand upon its side said, "Ah, the elephant is a wall." Another who felt its tail, exclaimed: "It is as a rope." Another one whose hand reached its ear, said: "It seems like a kind of fan." As for another blind man, whose hand was upon its leg, said, the elephant was:

"A pillar, like a tree-trunk." The last felt its tusk, stating the elephant is, "Hard, smooth, and like a spear."

The moral of the story is this: no one view gives you the accurate picture. Humans have a natural tendency to claim absolute truth based on their limited, subjective experience. However, oftentimes it takes multiple data points to give you the most accurate understanding.

The same is true with people analysis. Like the five senses, our research indicates a truer picture can be gained by the combination of certain scientifically validated assessments and applying them together for maximum advantage.

In Search Of The Best Assessments

When Dr. Alessandra and team began searching for the right solution, the goal was clear: identify those core and central elements of human behavior and cognition that have the greatest impact on professional performance. Alessandra knew already that the success in relationships was fundamentally based on The Platinum Rule—treating others as they want and need to be treated—and he wanted to be sure that extended into more than just behavioral understanding and communication.

The search began with a skeptical eye, and many personality assessments were quickly dismissed as little more than junk science. Objective personality testing began looking for maladjusted people, beginning with Woodworth's Personal Data Sheet in 1917, developed to identify soldiers prone to nervous breakdowns during enemy bombardment in World War I. (Today, we would term it posttraumatic stress disorder, but back then it was called shell shock.) With more than 2,500 assessments to examine, most were eliminated as not being scientifically validated or applicable for the real world in a way that was powerful and meaningful.

The team's research was looking for stable measurements of traits that would not change drastically or significantly in unexplained ways over time. The assessments needed to be normative in nature, meaning one individual's scores could be compared against another. Assessments needed to be highly reliable, which means they produce the same results if the same person takes them again and again. Finally, the assessments needed to be valid predictors of performance and descriptive enough to provide value to those taking them and reviewing the results.

The hunt was on to find the best assessments to identify behavioral and motivational styles first and then to account for and add in additional helpful and useful information to take some of the guesswork out of understanding the self and others. Assessments were compared and ranked. Some emerged through consensus that provided exactly what the team was hoping to find.

The Hunt To Identify Behavioral Styles

By far, DISC is the world's number one behavior profiling tool. DISC provides a highly detailed analysis of each person's natural (i.e., personal/ internal) and adapted (i.e., workplace/external) behavior styles. An individual's behavior is one of the strongest indicators of predictable response, emotional expression, and relationship fit whether that be in a particular job, a partnership, as the member of a team, or a leader in an organization.

In essence, DISC provides a predictable framework for how a person will likely behave in a given role or situation. Likewise, it offers the prescriptive insight necessary to maximize the outcome of any workplace or interpersonal interaction.

While the idea of four personality types dates back to ancient Greece and Hippocrates' Temperaments (Sanguine, Phlegmatic, Choleric and Melancholic), systematic people analytics is a twentieth century advancement that has come a long way since style typing was based on ancient medical concepts examining fluids in the body.

In 1928, Dr. William Moulton Marston published a book, *The Emotions of Normal People*, in which he described the theory that was validated during his studies at Harvard University. Marston defined four quadrants of personality, which are now commonly known as Dominance, Influence, Steadiness, and Conscientiousness.

In the 1940s, Walter V. Clarke, an industrial psychologist, was the first person to build an assessment instrument using Marston's theories; the Activity Vector Analysis was a checklist of adjectives on which he asked people to mark descriptors they identified as true of themselves. In the 1950s, along with John Cleaver, Clarke published the DISC questionnaire called "Self *Disc*ription," the first forced-choice version of DISC. In the 1970s, John Geier used that same tool to create the original Personal Profile System and collected data on 15 classical patterns of behaviors that are still currently used.

Many versions of assessments are used to measure behavioral tendencies based on the DISC model today. The original four quadrants (D, I, S, and C) based on Marston's model are still used for behavior profiling, though some modifications to the language and descriptors have developed a bit over the last century.

The Hunt To Identify Motivational Styles

Using DISC alone, though an incredible tool, only scratches the surface of what assessments can offer individuals and organizations. Motivators is the perfect companion assessment to pair with DISC. It measures the Seven Universal Dimensions of Motivation that drive each of us: *Aesthetic, Economic, Individualistic, Power, Altruistic, Regulatory, and Theoretical.* Just as DISC predicts how a person will behave, Motivators explains why people are compelled to do what they do.

Motivators combines the research of Dr. Eduard Spranger and Dr. Gordon Allport into a single, in-depth diagnostic tool, revealing the inherent motivations of each user. Dr. Spranger originally evaluated personalities in terms of six ideals or value orientations: theoretical, economic, aesthetic, social, political, and religious traits. His insight contributed to the understanding of motivation in his 1928 book, *Types of Men*. Allport was one of the first psychologists to focus on the study of the personality. As a Harvard University professor, he is often referred to as one of the founding figures of personality psychology and is the author of the 1937 classic, *Personality: A Psychological Interpretation*.

While most people are aware of their motivations to some degree, research shows that successful people share the common trait of exceptional self-awareness. Exceptional self-awareness means these individuals are better at recognizing opportunities that correlate with their inherent motivation and passions, thereby increasing their likelihood for success.

Likewise, leaders are better equipped to make informed personnel decisions when they understand what satisfies each new job applicant or team member. Knowing what drives people can be a game-changer in creating satisfaction and effectiveness in a variety of situations and relationships.

The Hunt To Identify Thinking Styles

Critical Thinking, based on the world-renowned Hartman Value Profile (HVP), offers a vital piece to the human puzzle. Based upon the research of Robert S. Hartman, this unique assessment measures an individual's problem-solving and processing skills, and their ability to avoid the blind spots associated with situational bias. The Critical Thinking assessment measures—with uncanny accuracy—an individual's critical thinking capacity, the ability to make balanced judgments, and one's decision-making skills.

Hartman was a logician and philosopher. His primary field of study was scientific axiology (the science of value) and he is known as its original theorist. He was also nominated for a Nobel Peace Prize in 1973. Based on his work, Assessments 24x7, in partnership with Viatech Global and Cornerstone Consulting, brought the HVP concepts to the Critical Thinking assessment, focusing specifically on how processing shows up in the workplace, and highlighting areas of strength and potential risk to be examined for relevancy in any situation. Through this simple and practical approach, individuals can see how their own blend of thinking and personal bias can impact their effectiveness.

The Critical Thinking assessment is not a psychological, intelligence, or aptitude test. Instead, the assessment objectively captures specific thinking patterns and documents the brain's natural selection process when making decisions, even at the subconscious level. Understanding the ways in which one processes information is directly linked to the ability to leverage strengths and limit potential performance blockers. A person's thinking and mental processing ability, like musical or sports talent, can be honed and improved but it takes thousands of hours and focused effort to create new neural pathways. Furthermore, to improve decision-making, individuals must first understand their unique blend of thinking style, their distinct biases, and their associated strengths or challenges of judgment as a result.

The Hunt To Identify Emotional IQ Styles

Emotional Intelligence (EIQ) helps users understand the correlation between the way they understand and apply their own emotions and the outcome of their interactions with others. This adds beautifully to the measures already discussed, as it is shown to improve decision-making, leadership ability, reading the emotions of others, and engaging in a greater number of mutually beneficial workplace and personal outcomes.

Most everyone has heard of the IQ (intelligence quotient) test. The first modern intelligence test was developed in 1904 and consisted of several components such as logical reasoning, finding rhyming words, and naming objects.

A new term, emotional intelligence, first appeared in a 1964 paper by Michael Beldoch and in a 1966 paper by B. Leuner entitled "Emotional Intelligence and Emancipation," which appeared in the psychotherapeutic journal, *Practice of Child Psychology and Child Psychiatry*. Howard Gardner's 1983 book, *Frames of Mind: The Theory of Multiple Intelligences*, introduced the idea that traditional types of intelligence, such as IQ, fail to fully explain cognitive ability. He introduced the idea of multiple intelligences, which included both interpersonal and intrapersonal intelligence.

In 1989, Stanley Greenspan put forward a model to describe emotional intelligence, followed by another from Peter Salovey and John Mayer published in the following year. The term became widely known with the publication of Daniel Goleman's 1995 book, *Emotional Intelligence: Why it can matter more than IQ.*

Unlike an individual's mostly fixed IQ, studies have demonstrated that emotional intelligence is malleable, coachable, and capable of being improved so it makes for an excellent awareness and improvement tool.

Backed by the strong quantifiable research evidence demonstrating its measurable professional value, the EIQ assessment provides evaluation and recommendations that assert all individuals are capable of improving their emotional intelligence and gleaning the powerful benefits that come with this heightened self-perspective.

The Big Picture

It's important to note that there are no right or wrong answers when it comes to assessments of this nature. In the end, the essential value in any assessment instrument is the extent to which it provides a useful indicator of an individual's preferences and patterns. These assessments produce insight to help us intentionally decide what is best in each situation, environment, or relationship. Ideally, this insight should encourage self-reflection and thoughtful consideration of whether any adjustments are either necessary or desirable.

For individuals, these assessments give a high level of intentional control over actions and responses so people can purposefully determine what is required in any circumstance, and adjust accordingly, while maintaining their own healthy balance of energy use.

From an organization's perspective, assessments can help management and leadership to reflect upon training and development strategies to ensure the greatest reach and support needed for the highest level of effectiveness in the organization. Assessments can help companies find the right people, understand how best to lead them, acknowledge their areas of development and strength, and encourage them to work better together as high-functioning teams. Assessments can help employees feel heard, seen, and valued as organizations invest in them. The assessments highlighted here work together seamlessly, providing data and insight to drive objective talent and management decisions and to build significant retention strategies.

Using well-validated, highly predictive assessments can give business leaders an important advantage when trying to manage employees and teams. This is why many of the world's top coaches and Fortune 500 executives rely on these assessments to ensure positive outcomes in the areas of employee selection, leadership development, sales and customer service training, team building, communication and collaboration training, conflict resolution, and succession planning.

One View Is Not Enough

By now it should be clear that one view is not enough. Using assessments in combination improves the ability to clearly see valid predictors of performance, communication outcomes, and decision choices in both personal and professional circumstances.

Knowing more about the assessments is helpful in determining how they can best be used to achieve results for your organization and your relationships. A more in-depth understanding will also improve your ability to increase the return on investment. Matching the assessment solution to the objective is the proper way to maximize the impact on the bottom line.

Additionally, these assessments and the information they reveal really can change lives. Beginning with building a solid foundation of self-awareness, any of these assessments can reveal more information to us about who we are and what we do, why we do it, and whether or not it works for us in the way we intend. These tools should be used to empower individuals to choose to live life by design rather than default.

If you understand what you are about and where it comes from, you can make a choice—decide to do things exactly as you are, or decide with educated intention that you want to do something differently. Not only can these tools help you to transform your own effectiveness and satisfaction as well as put you in a position of greater self-control and knowingness, but you will also see countless benefits to your interactions with others.

Understanding the self comes first, and then we can determine the best ways for us to create more connection with others, deepen relationships, and support or guide others in their own growth and development. We can actively seek to become the best versions of ourselves, and encourage and influence others to do the same.

Each assessment deserves a deeper dive to understand the nuances, to comprehend how it accomplishes what it does, and provide illustrative cases of the assessments in action. The following chapters examine each of the assessments in greater depth. After an examination of the assessments, there is an example of application. For some people, this logically includes becoming certified in the use of the assessments, which is something Assessments 24x7 excels in providing.

APPLYING ASSESSMENT SCIENCE

Best Ways To Use Assessments

For optimal results, assessments should be used in combination to decipher a more comprehensive picture of employees. This is critical for team building, conflict resolution, candidate selection, and succession planning.

Here are ten of the top ways to use assessments:

1. **Improve employee training and workshops.** Validated assessments are a great foundation to build programs for development.

2. **Improve employee coaching.** When coaches understand the person they are working with, they can tailor approaches to maximize success.

3. **Get the right people in the right roles.** Assessments help managers know the strengths and weaknesses of team members.

4. **Provide managers and employees a common language.** The language of the assessments can improve team communications.

5. **Make managers better leaders.** Because there are no right or wrong answers to assessments, just different styles, managers can become better leaders. Armed with this knowledge, managers can do more to motivate teams, communicate change, and delegate effectively.

6. **Improve hiring.** Assessments can uncover a tremendous amount of valuable information about how an

employee will interact with others, respond to stress, and handle problem-solving.

7. **Effectively manage difficult team members.** Assessments can diagnose potential sources of workplace conflict. Prevention is the best approach.

8. **Select better teams.** There is more to team success than just finding the best people for the team. Team success is often dependent on how the team members work together.

9. **Select better leaders.** Assessments help reveal the real, objective measures of great leadership. Once strengths and weaknesses are revealed, leaders can be trained and coached to improve.

10. **Set employees up for success.** Using assessments to truly understand the person goes a long way toward workplace satisfaction, improving retention, and increasing productivity.

Identifying And Exploring Behavioral Styles: DISC Assessment

Misunderstanding behavior is a disease that
afflicts the human race.

We are are a society struggling in disagreements, false impressions, and misinterpretations about people's behavior. It's paralyzing when we consider how fundamentally important it is for people to live in shared communities and our basic need for human connection.

With nearly 7.8 billion unique individuals on the planet, a lack of understanding of human behavior should come as no surprise. The real wonder is how we communicate at all, much less understand one another's behavior and emotions. This is an age-old dilemma. People have sought to better understand human behavior for various reasons for thousands of years.

What could a better understanding of human behavior and emotion do for you? You may hope to build partnerships, create friendships, move projects forward, reach goals that involve others, or build a stronger community. That is the positive side, but there is also the negative. All of us have had the misfortune of being upset or frustrated because we are unable to connect or communicate with someone else.

From the simplest of interactions to the most complex transactions, there is always an opportunity for miscommunication and misunderstanding. It can happen even when we have the best intentions, simply because we are all different and we tend to see the world from our viewpoint.

The good news is science has produced a validated way to help us better understand human behavior and emotions and live by The Platinum Rule—treating others as they want and need to be treated.

The DISC Quest To Better Understand Human Behavior

It is true that people see the world through their own set of lenses.

It is true that people expect the things they understand and value will also be understood and valued by others. But it doesn't always work that way, does it?

Even without trying to cause trouble, sometimes we find ourselves unable to communicate effectively or get what we need. We try our best, but we get stuck. What happened? What did we miss? What did we get wrong?

Wouldn't it be great if we could build more rapport and alleviate tension with others? Would it change our world if we could understand and communicate in ways that really worked?

The DISC model (with the title based on the acronym for the four behavior styles: Dominance, Influence, Steadiness, Conscientiousness) is designed to do exactly that—create a context of understanding that is simple, practical, and applicable to help us identify and respond to the needs, fears, emotions, and behaviors of others in a way that strengthens our connections rather than limits them. Through classifications that are easy to understand and remember, DISC seeks to provide a predictable and systematic framework of behaviors and ways of expressing emotion that can be used to identify a person's behavioral patterns and teach us to adapt appropriately. With these skills, we can work to decrease tension and increase effectiveness in all relationships by providing a look into our own experiences and patterns based on a snapshot of a moment in time.

Understanding Each Other Is The Key To Connection

Consider this scenario:

Charles, an engineer, is organized and controlled. In DISC terms, you will learn Charles has predominantly expressed C style behaviors. Charles is the epitome of being conscientious. He prides himself on being a perfectionist at heart and takes his time to complete tasks accurately. Charles likes to research things thoroughly, does his homework, and is always prepared. Charles, like any other C style, hates to be criticized.

Ian, the highly personable sales manager of the company, has a marketing issue to discuss with Charles. In DISC terminology, you will learn Ian is predominantly an I style. Ian succeeds in sales because he is influential and charismatic. Because he understands DISC, Ian knows he should not start the conversation with Charles by sharing stories about his great weekend, his new boat, and the vacation he has planned. Being open like that is great for an I like Ian, but not the way a C like Charles wants to be treated.

Instead, to make the right connection, Ian gets right to the point and the task. Ian starts out by making it clear he appreciates Charles' attention to detail and diligent efforts and he is seeking out Charles to help find the right solution to the marketing issue. To prevent Charles from becoming resentful about the issue Ian wants to discuss, Ian frames the issue as a variable that is out of Charles' control and not a personal attack of him or his work so far. To do otherwise might risk Charles avoiding future interactions with Ian. In addition, Ian promises to provide Charles with all the data he needs to analyze the problem and come up with a mutually acceptable and accurate solution.

While it is necessary for Ian to adapt his behavior for this interaction, it is also important that Ian gets what he needs from the connection. By working with Charles in a way that meets his needs and fears, Ian is effectively getting the solution to his problem, and building a stronger professional relationship with Charles.

Learning to understand each other and creating mutually beneficial relationships is the key to successful connection.

Misunderstanding DISC

Unlike what you may have heard before:

- DISC assessments are not intelligence tests.

- DISC assessments don't measure education or experience.

- DISC assessments are not indicators of values.

- DISC assessments do not provide judgment of right and wrong behavior.

- DISC assessments are not predictors of how *well* we do things, just *how* we do them.

In truth, DISC is simply a tool for identifying and understanding human behavior and emotion.

The DISC assessment and report tools offer an in-depth identification of individual style tendencies in four behavioral styles widely-known as Dominance, Influence, Steadiness, and Conscientiousness. DISC reports also provide a comprehensive view of behavioral style blends. Information from the DISC assessment is based on self-perception and offers a snapshot of a moment in time as well as a benchmark of more instinctual behaviors. The DISC report provides an overview and explores two different viewpoints—the natural style (who we are when left to all our own choices without the influence of others) and the adapted style (how we think we need to behave to be effective in the situation, environment, or relationship). In other words, our natural style reveals the behaviors that we adopt easily when faced with no limitations, and our adapted style reveals our preferred behaviors when we are faced with circumstantial expectations or constraints.

Furthermore, the DISC report offered by Assessments 24x7 outlines a series of adaptability resources and practice opportunities to apply your new knowledge in a variety of circumstances. With just one tool, you can easily begin to understand yourself, and those around you, to create stronger connections.

DISC CONCERNS AND RESOLUTIONS

- **DISC isn't always 100% accurate.**
  DISC is not all-knowing; people are complex and can't be described with just one assessment. There may be tendencies that don't fit 100% because humans are multi-faceted and we can't always capture every detail in a short report.

- **DISC doesn't look at the values that drive our decisions and actions.**
  The values that drive our decisions and actions are measured through other assessment instruments like Motivators and Hartman Value Profile.

- **DISC doesn't cover critical thinking attributes much.**
  DISC doesn't fully examine critical thinking skills and decision-making, but provides an opportunity for those things to be explored based on behavioral tendencies.

- **DISC is a stereotyping tool.**
  DISC is not meant to be a model to put people in a box and stereotype them. We are all behavioral blends, so this tool provides insights to help us learn to communicate and interact more effectively.

- **Once I understand DISC, that's all I need to know.**
  Making assumptions and judgments is never appropriate, whether based on the basic DISC model or otherwise. Without fully understanding the nuances of how multiple elements function in combination with other measures we are likely to get it wrong. While it can be a starting point, it is never intended to be used as the only resource or tool.

- **I shouldn't have to take the assessment more than once.**
  DISC is not a one and done product. Remember, it's a snapshot of a moment in time, and our adapted styles can change moment to moment, though the natural style typically stays more consistent.

The History Of DISC

DISC theories, strategies, and tactics are not new. The idea of measuring and classifying temperaments into four distinct categories has been around for a long time.

While the language and descriptors have changed, the four primary types have a great deal of consistency over time. Here is a breakdown of how some of the foundations and language of DISC has evolved through the ages:

	D	I	S	C
Hippocrates Humors— 400BC	Choleric	Sanguine	Phlegmatic	Melancholic
Aristotle Elements— 350BC	Air	Fire	Water	Earth
Carl Jung Functions— 1921	Extroverted/ Thinking/ Sensing	Extroverted/ Feeling/ Intuiting	Introverted/ Feeling/ Intuiting	Introverted/ Thinking/ Sensing
William Marston Primary Emotions— 1928	Dominance	Inducement	Submission	Compliance
Walter Clarke Vectors— 1940s	Aggressive	Sociable	Stable	Avoidant
Assessments 24x7 Behavioral Styles—1970s	Dominance	Influence	Steadiness	Conscien- tiousness

The current model of DISC and the associated assessment tool, based on the theory of psychologist William Moulton Marston, centers on what he called the primary emotions: Dominance, Inducement, Submission, and Compliance, though the names have been modified. He asserted that normal people (those who are not under the influence of abnormal psychological circumstances, like mental illness, for example) had predictable responses to various stimuli and offered his theory in the 1928 book, *The Emotions of Normal People*. He urged that these behavioral types came from a sense of self and interaction with the environment.

Marston included two dimensions that influenced emotional behavior. The first dimension is whether a person views the environment as favorable or unfavorable. The second dimension is whether a person perceives having control or lack of control over the environment.

Here is a quick summary of the four descriptors of DISC he outlined, with the currently used titles:

D is for Dominance. Perceives oneself as *more powerful* than the environment and perceives the environment as *unfavorable.*

I is for Influence. Perceives oneself as *more powerful* than the environment and perceives the environment as *favorable.*

S is for Steadiness. Perceives oneself as *less powerful* than the environment and perceives the environment as *favorable.*

C is for Conscientiousness. Perceives oneself as *less powerful* than the environment and perceives the environment as *unfavorable.*

Marston's work was the foundation of the DISC assessment that has been used by more than 50 million people since it was first introduced in 1972, and it is still the compass for understanding behavior and emotions today.

Marston never created a formal assessment, but his theory was then developed into a behavioral assessment tool by psychologist Walter Vernon Clarke that measured how individuals perceived themselves and how they thought others would perceive them. Named the Activity Vector Analysis, it was a checklist of adjectives asking people to indicate descriptions that were accurate about themselves. The assessment was originally intended for use in businesses needing assistance in choosing qualified employees.

Nearly ten years later, Clarke Associates developed a new version of this instrument with John Cleaver called the "Self-*Discr*iption" and instead of using a checklist, this version forced respondents to make a choice between two applicable terms noting *most* and *least* descriptive. This process is still in use today, though there have been adjustments to the instrument with the word choices and descriptions.

In the 1970s, further analysis of the assessment added to the support of a DISC-based instrument. "Self-*Disc*ription" was used by John Geier, PhD and Dorothy Downey to create the original Personal Profile System (PPS). Using the data from the twenty-four-question forced responses, Geier and Downey created a clearer version, and the DISC assessment tool, in its original version, was born.

Understanding The DISC Model

DISC is a simple, practical, easy to remember, and universally applicable model of understanding needs-motivated, observable behavior and emotion. It combines awareness of nature (the inherent) and nurture (the learned) characteristics and reveals behavioral tendencies in natural and adapted styles.

D = Dominance	How people address problems and challenges
I = Influence	How people handle situations involving people and contacts
S = Steadiness	How people demonstrate pace and consistency
C = Conscientiousness	How people react to procedures and constraints

DISC measures the intensity of characteristics using scales of directness and openness (direct/indirect and guarded/open). It also looks at these through descriptors of pace and priority.

Imagine this scenario:

Sharon, a director of HR at a tech company, values harmony and is an excellent peacemaker. In DISC, she is an S. Steady Sharon is her nickname at the company. She wants everyone to be happy and strives to create a positive work environment. She also is known for being the go-to for support and one of the hardest workers in the group.

A department leader at the company, Dave, has a dominant behavioral style. In DISC, he would show as an expressed D style. There is a risk of a Dominance style like Dave confronting a Steadiness style, like Sharon, head-on with a problem. Sharon may feel threatened and withdraw from the perceived conflict. Sharon might agree to make a change to keep the peace between them, but she may be resistant to follow-through with the request.

Through DISC training, Dave learned when he talks to an S like Sharon about a problem, he needs to start by focusing on things they agree on and trying to soften his style. Instead of a "my way or the highway" approach, Dave makes a connection with Sharon by framing his request kindly, and explaining how it will improve company harmony and morale. By recognizing Sharon's needs and fears, Dave can more easily get what he needs while effectively connecting with Sharon.

Below, you can see the differences for each style in directness and openness, and pace and priority.

DIRECTNESS AND OPENNESS OF EACH STYLE

STYLE	TENDENCIES
DOMINANCE	Tends to be direct and guarded
INFLUENCE	Tends to be direct and open
STEADINESS	Tends to be indirect and open*
CONSCIENTIOUSNESS	Tends to be indirect and guarded

*Important note: The S style is open to others, but the true emotion of the style is concealed. S styles are quite closed with their own emotions and you may never really know what they are experiencing; they are concerned with their safety if their true self becomes exposed. The S style, therefore, appears open, but it is not really open at all.

PACE AND PRIORITY OF EACH STYLE

STYLE	TENDENCIES
DOMINANCE	Fast-paced and task-oriented
INFLUENCE	Fast-paced and people-oriented
STEADINESS	Slow-paced and people-oriented
CONSCIENTIOUSNESS	Slow-paced and task-oriented

To help create an even clearer picture of the distinctions in behavior for each style, the following behavioral descriptors are useful for understanding the DISC model:

DOMINANCE	INFLUENCE	STEADINESS	CONSCIENTIOUSNESS
Decisive	Charming	Understanding	Accurate
Competitive	Confident	Friendly	Precise
Daring	Convincing	Good Listener	Analytical
Direct	Enthusiastic	Patient	Compliant
Innovative	Inspiring	Relaxed	Courteous
Persistent	Optimistic	Sincere	Diplomatic
Adventurous	Persuasive	Stable	Detailed
Problem Solver	Sociable	Steady	Fact Finder
Results Oriented	Trusting	Team Player	Objective

It is helpful to remember there may be descriptors in more than one style that align with our behavior. That's okay! We are all a blend of all four DISC styles, and we can have tendencies in more than one style at a time.

Some people have secondary DISC styles that are very close to their primary styles as well, which may have significant influences on their behavior that are supportive or contrary. For example, if I am a very high S and C with close scores, my pace is likely to be much slower overall because they are both slower-paced styles. My focus will shift from people to task, though, because the priority for each style is different. This brings another level of complexity to our human expression of behavior and emotion.

To help bring additional clarity, let's continue to explore these styles individually.

Dominance Styles

Dominance styles are driven by two governing needs: to control and achieve. People who predominantly possess the D style are goal-oriented go-getters who are most comfortable when they are in charge of others and situations. They want to accomplish many things—right now—so they focus on no-nonsense approaches to bottom-line results.

Dominance styles seek expedience and are not afraid to bend the rules. They figure it is easier to seek forgiveness than to ask permission. Dominance styles accept challenges, take authority, and plunge head-first into solving problems. They work quickly and impressively by themselves, which means they become annoyed with delays. They are driven and dominating and can be stubborn, impatient, and insensitive to others as a result.

D | Strengths And Challenges

What Do They Do Best?

- Take charge, competitive, get things done
- Decisive risk-takers, visionary
- Fearless—no obstacle is too big to overcome
- Ensuring bottom-line results

What's Hard for Them?

- Repetitiveness—doing the same tasks over and over
- Being diplomatic—can come on strong in conversations
- Lots of rules and regulations
- Opening up—not shy, but private about personal matters

Influence Styles

People with predominant Influence styles are friendly, enthusiastic, charismatic people who like to be where the action is. They thrive on the admiration, acknowledgment, and compliments that come with being in the limelight. Their primary strengths are enthusiasm, charm, persuasiveness, and warmth. They are idea people and dreamers who excel at getting others excited about their vision.

Influence styles are eternal optimists with an abundance of magnetism. These qualities help them influence people and build alliances to accomplish their goals. Influence styles do have their weaknesses: impatience, an aversion to being alone, a lack of follow-through, and a short attention span. They are risk-takers who base many of their decisions on intuition and emotion, which is not inherently bad. They are not inclined to verify information; they are more likely to assume someone else will do it.

Strengths And Challenges

What Do They Do Best?
- Inspire others to take action, trusting
- Think fast on their feet—optimistic, intuitive, creative
- Full of ideas, but can be impulsive in trying them
- Promoting ideas, opportunities, or people

What's Hard for Them?
- Restrictions or routines
- Formal reports or keeping detailed records
- Routine—easily bored
- Staying focused on something through to conclusion

Steadiness Styles

Those with primary Steadiness styles are warm and nurturing individuals. They are the most people-focused of the four styles. Steadiness styles are excellent listeners, devoted friends, and loyal employees. Their relaxed disposition makes them approachable and warm. They develop strong networks of people who are willing to be mutually supportive and reliable.

Steadiness styles are excellent team players and risk-averse. In fact, Steadiness styles may tolerate unpleasant environments rather than risk change. They like the status quo and become distressed when disruptions occur. When faced with change, they think it through, plan how to make it successful, and then accept it into their world.

Steadiness styles, more than the other types, strive to maintain personal composure, predictability, stability, and balance. They are courteous, friendly, and willing to share responsibilities. They are good planners, persistent workers, and will follow through. They go along with others even when they do not agree because they do not want to rock the boat or cause any discomfort for others. They are slower decision-makers because of their need for security and safety, their need to avoid unnecessary risk, and their desire to include others in the process. S styles look for ways to bring consistency and predictability to their decisions, using their own personal criteria typically determined more with the heart (feelings) than with the head (objective data).

S | Strengths And Challenges

What Do They Do Best?
- Bring harmony to group situations
- Friendly and sensitive—great listeners
- Build networks of friends to help do work
- Coordinating and cooperating with others

What's Hard for Them?
- Competition
- Working with dictatorial or unfriendly people
- Making big decisions quickly—dislike sudden change
- Voicing contrary opinions, sharing emotions

Conscientiousness Styles

Those who are predominantly Conscientiousness styles are analytical, persistent, systematic people who enjoy complex problem-solving. C styles are detail-oriented, which makes them more concerned with content and accuracy than style. They are task-oriented people who enjoy perfecting processes and working toward tangible results. They're always in control of their emotions and may become uncomfortable around people who are very outgoing or seem flighty or easily distracted.

Conscientiousness styles have high expectations of themselves and others, which can make them overly critical. Their tendency toward perfectionism, taken to an extreme, can cause "analysis paralysis." C styles make decisions deliberately and slowly, thoroughly weighing pros and cons. They do research, make comparisons, determine risks, and calculate margins of error, and when they are sure it is all just right, they take action.

Conscientiousness styles become irritated by surprises and glitches, hence their cautious decision-making. C styles are also skeptical and likely to investigate data and resources to be sure everything they hear or see is correct.

 **C** | **Strengths And Challenges**

What Do They Do Best?
- Highly organized; they even plan spontaneity
- Plan thoroughly before deciding to act
- Quick thinking, but slow to speak
- Planning to meet specified expectations

What's Hard for Them?
- Working with unpredictable people or in disorganized environments
- Being outgoing/open—closed about personal matters
- Working with others or in groups—prefer to work alone
- Incomplete/unclear directions

The Needs, Fears, And Emotions Of Each Style

Our relationships rely on recognizing what other styles need and fear, and understanding how people will respond emotionally to one another. The goal is to build mutually beneficial relationships and that requires seeing what's under the surface of each style.

Following the principles of DISC and The Platinum Rule, you can refer to the DISC Focus chart (page 43) to help you easily understand what helps you work more effectively with others (and why others may be different from you). If we understand these elements, two things can happen:

1. We can approach every interaction with a curious and non-judgmental mindset knowing we are all unique and may see things differently

2. We can alleviate emotionally-charged interactions and respond in a way that helps us honor and respect one another so we all get what we need and want in a way that works

The needs and fears of DISC are driving forces for behavioral expression. We are likely to be influenced by our needs and fears according to our expressed behavioral styles, with our primary styles showing up most frequently. Furthermore, the connection to needs, fears, and emotions is more specifically linked to the predominant natural style that we primarily identify with and express.

Let's look at these styles one-by-one to see what might happen:

- If I am predominantly a D style, my go-to emotion will likely be one of anger, impatience, and urgency, particularly when things are not going my way. Because my needs and fears regarding control and challenge are being activated, my emotional reaction will be predominantly a D response to resolve the circumstance immediately and I'll become quite directive.

- If I am predominantly an I style, my go-to emotion will likely be one of optimism and trust in relationships to see me through whatever I'm facing. Because my needs and fears for connection and approval are being activated, I will likely respond emotionally as an I, looking for the silver lining, believing everything will work out, and creating opportunity for interaction and connection.

- If I am predominantly an S style, my go-to emotion will likely be one of patience and non-expression (I likely have emotions pumping under the surface, but I will not show them to anyone). Because my needs and fears around safety and stability are activated, I will likely respond from an S style perspective, offering patience and support, considering the impact on others, and focusing on how I can keep things as steady as possible for everyone.

- If I am predominantly a C style, my go-to emotion will likely be one of fear and concern that whatever needs to be done is done right and within the constraints and rules. Because my needs and fears for accuracy and quality are activated, I will likely respond as a C style, looking for ways to correct what needs attention, increasing quality and exactness, and adhering to procedures and rules.

	D	**I**	**S**	**C**
DISC Focus	Problems/ Constraints	People/ Contacts	Pace/ Consistency	Procedures/ Constraints
Needs	Challenges to solve, authority	Social relationships, friendly environment	Systems, teams, stable environment	Rules to follow, data to analyze
Fears	Being taken advantage of/ loss of control	Being left out/ loss of social approval	Sudden change/ loss of stability and security	Being criticized/ loss of accuracy and quality
Emotions	Anger, impatience	Optimism, trust	Patience, non-expression	Fear, concern

It is incredibly important to remember that because many of us are a blend of styles, we may have blended needs, fears, and emotions. For example, a high D and high I style combination will likely experience some irritation and impatience, followed by optimism and believing things will be ok. She may think, "this is so frustrating, but I know it will work out in the end."

Focus On Emotions

Recognizing and understanding the emotions of each style is one of the greatest resources DISC offers.

All people are emotional creatures and will experience and express emotions.

While emotions are a combination of response to stimulus and our attitudes about what we need and if that will be met or not, our emotional responses are often somewhat predictable, based on our behavioral style. As mentioned before, most of us are a blend of expressed styles, so more than one emotion may be present and our emotions may shift depending on environment, situation, or relationship. However, particularly in heightened stress, we will behave in our natural style tendencies more often.

The table above outlines the four primary emotions of DISC:

- D = Anger and impatience

- I = Optimism and trust

- S = Patience and non-expression

- C = Fear and concern

As with the behaviors of DISC, these are measured in highs and lows, and the associated expressions are opposites.

- A high D will respond emotionally with anger and impatience, as a low D will respond by becoming more agreeable and cooperative, and will exhibit patience for the circumstance and situation.

- A high I will look through an optimistic lens and exhibit trust in others to help in emotional circumstances, while a low I will take a more realistic or even pessimistic look at the situation, and be slow to involve and trust others.

- A high S will offer a great deal of patience and control, often not showing emotions, while a low S will be more likely to wear emotions on their sleeves and easily express everything they are feeling.

- A high C, being very committed to doing things right, and not being caught doing it wrong, will comply with a strong level of caution and inflexibility while a low C style is likely to take more risks, dismiss the rules as guidelines, and express a flexible attitude.

DISC Styles Under Stress

When experiencing stress, the DISC styles will often have specific expressions of their behavior and emotions. These tendencies are driven by our highest natural style because in stress, humans respond out of instinct (fight, flight, or freeze) and our natural behavioral tendency is an instinctual behavior expression. When examining behavior and emotion under stress, it is helpful to know that these instinctual responses are often disproportionate to logic, fueled by emotion, and an effort to relieve the tension we feel within our person as our styles come to life. The needs, fears, and emotions we've discussed can be on hyperdrive as we seek to relieve that tension as quickly as possible.

Furthermore, our perception of how we are behaving under stress can be very different than how others perceive our behaviors.

It's been said that we judge ourselves on our intentions and others on their behavior.

If someone is not clear on our intention and only sees the expression of behavior, they may misunderstand why we do what we do, particularly in stress. It is also important to note that stress can build up over time or upon itself in long-term stressful experiences, which may cause even more extreme expression if it continues and isn't managed appropriately.

More About Each Style

The chart on the following page will help you understand some of the characteristics of each of the four basic DISC styles, so you can interact with each style more effectively. It is useful in describing how a person behaves and is perceived in personal, social, and work situations. Keep in mind, these descriptors are for the high intensity of each style, so you can modify them according to level (i.e., those low in a style will likely have the opposite style's characteristics).

	HIGH DOMINANT STYLE	HIGH INFLUENCING STYLE	HIGH STEADY STYLE	HIGH CONSCIENTIOUS STYLE
Tends to Act	Assertive	Persuasive	Supportive	Analytical
When in Conflict, this Style	Demands action	Attacks	Complies	Avoids
Needs	Control	Approval	Routine	Standards
Primary Drive	Independence	Interaction	Stability	Correctness
Preferred Tasks	Challenging	People related	Scheduled	Structured
Comfortable With	Being decisive	Social friendliness	Being part of a team	Order and planning
Personal Strength	Problem-solver	Encourager	Supporter	Organizer
Strength Overextended	Preoccupation on goals over people	Speaking without thinking	Procrastination in addressing change	Overanalyzing everything
Personal Limitation	Too direct and intense	Too disorganized and nontraditional	Too indecisive and indirect	Too detailed and impersonal
Personal Wants	Control, variety	Approval, less structure	Routine, harmony	Standards, logic
Personal Fear	Losing Control	Social Rejection	Sudden Change	Being Wrong
Blind Spots	Being held accountable	Follow-through on commitments	Embracing need for change	Struggle to make decisions without overanalyzing
Needs to Work On	Empathy, patience	Controlling emotions, follow-through	Being assertive when pressured	Worrying less about everything
Measuring Maturity	Giving up control	Objectively handling rejection	Standing up for self when confronted	Not being defensive when criticized
Under Stress May Become	Dictatorial, critical	Sarcastic, superficial	Submissive, indecisive	Withdrawn, headstrong
Measures Worth By	Impact or results, track record	Acknowledgments, compliments	Compatibility, contributions	Precision, accuracy, quality of results

Understanding The Styles: Expressed Versus Concealed Behaviors

Once we have an understanding of how each style operates and functions individually, the next critical perspective is looking at how the four styles come together to create our behavioral blend. When looking at a report, there are a few things to consider when it comes to the scores of our D, I, S, and C.

Expressed behaviors are those tendencies with which we engage and show to the world, often with the greatest intensity. Concealed behaviors are those that are the opposite of expressed.

While an expressed behavior will be easily seen by others, a concealed behavior may not come out as frequently or may not be revealed at all.

Another way to think of expressed and concealed behaviors is that expressed behaviors truly engage the tendencies of the style, but a concealed behavior will resist the style, or express the opposite of the style. For example, a high D style expresses the behaviors of a high D—assertive, dominant, decisive. A low D style expresses the opposite of the D behaviors, resisting the D style—passive, submissive, agreeable. This idea of expressed and concealed behavior is another way to remember that the DISC model tendencies are polarized; the high and low behavior descriptors are opposites.

It is common to have multiple styles that we express and multiple styles we conceal in our behavior. It is less common to only have one expressed style and three concealed behavioral styles, and much more common to have more than one style expressed or more than one style concealed. Remember, with any DISC blend, we can shift our styles at any time to engage or resist a style tendency.

To take it one step further, if we use our natural style as a baseline measure of our tendencies for behavior, and compare our adapted style to it, we can determine if we are shifting our styles from expressed to concealed or vice versa. This can help us clearly see why our behavior changes depending on the situation, environment, or relationship.

Intensity Of DISC Styles

The intensity of the DISC styles is also correlated to the expressed and concealed behaviors. Styles that score higher on the scale are aligned with expressed behaviors, whereas lower-scoring styles are aligned with concealed behaviors. One way to think about intensity is that the closer you are to a score of fifty (the midline or center), the more your behaviors in this style will be balanced or situational. Another way to see it is that the higher your score, the more you will actively behave as the descriptors of the style (high D will behave as we would expect a D to behave) and the lower your score, the more you will likely behave as the opposite of what we would expect from that style (low D will be submissive and agreeable, not like a D style would be expected to behave).

Another key to the intensity of styles is the very high and very low scores; scores over 90 are considered overextended, while scores under 10 are considered underextended. In either case, whether very high or very low, these scores have a specific connection to the DISC style—the behavioral tendency associated becomes a need versus a want. When styles become extreme, either high or low, the person will create an environment where those behavioral needs can be met. Because of the intensity of the style, if the score is over or underextended, the behavior must fulfill that need.

This is especially helpful to understand so we can recognize the behaviors for what they are, an expression of needs, and know how we can best adapt to others when necessary. When people have extreme scores, it takes more time, energy, and attention for them to adapt to others who are not like them. If we know they have an over or underextended score, we can be more diligent in adapting to them versus expecting them to adapt easily to us.

D = Dominance

- Over 90—Needs to win and dominate, "warrior spirit" fights for survival
- Under 10—Needs to be agreeable, submissive, and yielding

I = Influence

- Over 90—Needs control and connections, maintains control by keeping people close
- Under 10—Needs protection from others, keeps people away

S = Steadiness

- Over 90—Needs safety, security, predictability
- Under 10—Needs commotion, possibilities, chaos, and risk

C = Conscientiousness

- Over 90—Needs accuracy and precision, being correct and right
- Under 10—Needs flexibility, openness, and nonconformity

Fifteen Classical DISC Patterns

As we build on this idea of how our styles come together, it's important to remember DISC isn't only about our individual styles of D, I, S, and C. These each combine for every person to create a unique DISC style blend that is determined primarily by our expressed styles.

Some blends are more common than others, and Clarke's work set the stage for Geier to identify the fifteen classical patterns of DISC. These patterns are still used today to further explain behavioral style blends.

Note: There are many more possible styles when combining the four DISC behavioral dimensions. The fifteen classic styles are naturally occurring groups that represent the primary behavioral style or characteristics observed by others when working and interacting in common work situations.

Fifteen DISC Style Behavioral Patterns
*Words in parentheses are the original classical pattern names attributed to John Geier.

- Finisher (Achiever)
- Harmonizer (Agent)
- Assessor (Appraiser)
- Coach (Counselor)
- Explorer (Creative)
- Producer (Developer)
- Dynamo (Inspirational)
- Examiner (Investigator)

- Fact-Finder (Objective Thinker)
- Formalist (Perfectionist)
- Influencer (Persuader)
- Technician (Practitioner)
- Networker (Promoter)
- Results-Driven (Results-Oriented)
- Planner (Specialist)

Finishers (Achievers)—SD styles possess a strong sense of personal accountability and results orientation. They will likely demonstrate a keen interest in the quality of the work being done. Because they have a high opinion for the quality of their own work, they can often either do a task themselves or take back a delegated task so it's done right. Finishers (Achievers) operate at a high efficiency and expect acknowledgement and rewards for their efforts.

Harmonizers (Agents)—SI styles balance interpersonal connections and goals/objectives. They are supportive, make others feel included, and extend a hand of friendship. They tend to be well organized and deliver effective results. Being service-oriented, the Harmonizer (Agent) style is quite good at taking on/helping with tasks that others may struggle with themselves. They do not like conflict and may avoid connections with assertive individuals.

Assessors (Appraisers)—IC styles apply creative focus to practical, workable concepts and make them doable. They display competitive and results-oriented interactions but engage others with persuasion rather than through aggressive methods. They are good at explaining their ideas and the steps required to reach their goals. They are organized and often have a step-by-step action plan to ensure a good result. Assessors (Appraisers) can be quite verbal in stating their dissatisfaction and criticizing others who are not contributing.

Coaches (Counselors)—IS styles are adept at solving people problems. They are seen as warm, empathetic, and insightful. They like to form extended personal relationships and often develop a reputation for unobtrusive, contributory efforts when working with others. Coaches (Counselors) can become too lenient with marginal contributors and tend to be too mild when issuing corrections, directions, and expectations.

Explorers (Creatives)—DC Styles display opposing directions in their behaviors. There is a desire for results and goal achievement and a competing desire for those results to be perfect. They shift between aggression and sensitivity, and the desire for immediate results vs. consideration of alternatives. They often make routine decisions quickly but may need to exercise caution for bigger ones. They are change agents who will want the space and flexibility to explore by retesting and revisiting their conclusions over time. Explorers (Creatives) can be seen as emotionally distant and sometimes surprisingly direct.

Producers (Developers)—D styles follow their own path and will seek new projects and challenges. They are self-reliant and like to solve their issues without asking for help. This independence fosters innovation that is strongly advocated to others. Being in control is important to them, and they can push back if challenged. They have high expectations of others and can be quite critical if expected results lag. Producers (Developers) can be seen as uncaring, and at times, difficult to work with.

Dynamos (Inspirationals)—DI styles will make an attempt to adjust or modify the thoughts and actions of others. They are good at understanding how to steer others toward a predetermined result. They will set the stage for the desired result before they verbalize that desire. Their strong persuasive skills can elicit cooperation from others, but sometimes create a feeling by others of being manipulated. Dynamos (Inspirationals) can be intimidating and can seek to override the decisions of others.

Examiners (Investigators)—SDC styles are steady, objective, and analytical. They are successful due to their strong persistence in pursuing their objectives. They can excel in complex and/or technical projects. They rely upon logic rather than emotion. They like working alone and do not feel the need to engage or be involved with others. Examiners (Investigators) can sometimes be viewed as lacking tact and/or warmth.

Fact-finders (Objective Thinkers)—C styles have highly developed quality control and critical thinking ability. They favor logic and facts, but also possess intuitive abilities that they will meld with the facts. Preparation is essential prior to action. They may appear shy but can work with others who have a similar high-quality focus. They avoid confrontational situations, and because they need to "get it right," can delay decisions. If Fact-finders (Objective Thinkers) make a mistake, they will likely research additional material to support their original choice.

Formalists (Perfectionists)—CS styles rely upon procedure and structure in all aspects of life. They are detail-oriented and seek perfection. They need to know the expectations and the timetable for their work. They can get bogged down in detail and will not rush important decisions. They will take a risk if they have the facts to support it. Formalists (Perfectionists) may be initially suspicious of personal compliments, praise, or flattery.

Influencers (Persuaders)—ID styles enjoy working with others. They are viewed as friendly, even as they seek to accomplish their personal goals. They often gain the respect and support of others. They aspire to positions of authority, and it is important that they look good to others. They like variety in their day. They can be too optimistic about others and tend to believe they can influence others more than they likely can. Influencers (Persuaders) often need analytical support to offset their tendency to proceed without all the facts.

Technicians (Practitioners)—CIS styles will seek projects in their area(s) of expertise. They constantly challenge their own work and results. They are likely knowledgeable in many areas. They are easy to work with unless their expertise is challenged. They are quality-oriented and expect strong results from themselves and others. They can become critical of others if they achieve poor results. At times, Technicians (Practitioners) can become too insistent on doing things a certain way.

Networkers (Promoters)—I styles have many personal contacts who support their efforts. They are outgoing, socially comfortable, and make friends with ease. They promote with enthusiasm and draw on their contacts to help them achieve their goals. They are quite optimistic, which can lead to misjudging others. They may not spend time considering negative consequences of their "gut feel" inclinations. Networkers (Promoters) can over-talk others as they pursue their objectives.

Results-Driven (Results-Oriented)—DI styles display strong self-confidence that may be viewed as arrogance. They will pursue options that challenge them to achieve goals. They like difficult tasks and unique opportunities, and seek positions of authority. They avoid constraints. Rules can be viewed as loose guidelines. They act quickly and can become impatient and critical with more methodical and analytical people. In the extreme, Results-Driven (Results-Oriented) can appear cool and abrasive to others.

Planners (Specialists)—S styles blend well with most others. Moderate behaviors (unobtrusive behavior) define this pattern. They will likely be considerate, helpful, and patient. They will build a solid relationship with a limited number of associates and are most effective in specialized areas of expertise. They will be well planned and consistent in performance, and do not like fire drills. Planners (Specialists) are good at contributing to projects and activities.

Shifting To An Adapted Style

To understand the shifting of styles, we must first start with an acknowledgement that there are two distinctions in examining our behavioral tendencies: the *natural style* and the *adapted style*.

Our Natural Style is who we are at our core, how we operate without the influence of situation or any expectations. Our Adapted Style is how we think we need to behave based on a specific situation. Natural tendencies are usually more consistent over a lifetime, though are affected in part by our seasons of life and emotional experiences. They may likely be different in different periods as our beliefs, attitudes, and life changes. Adapted tendencies are a snapshot of how you see yourself in a particular activity, focus, or environment and can change quickly and regularly as we adjust to those environments, situations, or relationships.

When we are clear on our own style makeup and how it all starts to come together as our blend, our effectiveness can depend on how we pay attention to our styles shifting from our natural to adapted tendencies. For some individuals, the DISC style stays consistent. They are less likely to shift their style depending on the situation, environment, or relationship. This can either be a strength or a limitation; the benefit is that they are who they are, no matter the circumstance. The downside is that sometimes that is not the most effective way to behave, and by not adapting, they may not be doing what's most appropriate for the situation, environment, or relationship.

On the other hand, many individuals adapt their DISC styles to their situations, environments, or relationships, depending on what they perceive the need to be in that moment. It may be a small adjustment— like being a little less open at work to maintain a professional distance with coworkers— or it may be a significant adjustment. For example, low C styles who are very flexible in their natural tendency but are HR representatives at work, may require more shifting and adapting to adhere strictly to policies and procedures (high C behavior).

Any amount of shifting can take energy. Some shifts are easier to make than others, and some shifts don't require as much energy. As a general rule, when someone's style shifts twenty points, whether an increase or decrease in the score, they are using a significant amount of energy. The extra energy used, especially if sustained over a long period of time, can have significant effects on their ability to continue to shift well and maintain their energy and stamina, and can cause things like burnout and exhaustion when not managed well.

So, is it better to be consistent in our style from natural to adapted, or better to shift? The answer is yes to both—sometimes being consistent with our styles is appropriate and effective, but other times, shifting is necessary for us to have the best potential outcomes. Rather than trying to determine if we should shift or should stay the same, it is much more essential to look at three things:

1. Does a shift make sense for the situation, environment, or relationship?

2. Is it necessary for me to shift to be as effective as possible?

3. Am I getting what I need by shifting my style and using my energy differently?

If the answer to any of these questions is no, then shifting may not be the best solution. Why use up your energy shifting your behavior if it doesn't make sense and doesn't make a difference?

If the answer to all these questions is yes, then shifting is likely the best choice. But once the shift to an adapted style has occurred, it's important to be mindful of how much energy that shift uses. If you find at the end of the day, week, or month you are exhausted, not in a fulfilling, content way, but downright over it and done, your energy shift is taking a lot out of you.

If the shift is necessary, you don't want to stop shifting because you may lose effectiveness. Instead, you need to find ways to manage the energy you use. Make time to recharge your batteries when you feel them draining. Pay extra attention to those days you feel are harder than others, and be attentive to your own needs. Rest, eat well, exercise, and do whatever you need to do to build up the energy you need, and sustain it at a healthy level to avoid running yourself into the ground with all you're accomplishing.

Adapting For Effectiveness

Remember it is important to recognize that our natural tendencies may not be as effective, given the needs of the environment, situation, or relationship, and we may need to adjust. Sometimes, our style may need to be modified slightly to help us address the needs, fears, and emotions of the circumstance or with others in order to create the most mutually beneficial experience or relationship possible.

This idea of adapting our style can be a bit daunting at times (and even confusing) as we seek to be as authentic as possible. There is nothing about adapting that requires us to compromise who we are or act in a way that is fake. Adapting to a different style is like dressing in the right clothing for the task at hand. You likely wouldn't wear a tuxedo or ball gown to weed the garden or wash the dog. Finding the best way to be effective with our behavioral style is similar. Sometimes, we may need to wear the best "style" for the job or task, knowing that we can change our approach to match the situation, but we are still ourselves under whatever outfit we may choose to wear in that moment.

The same thing is true in communication. We are still ourselves at our core, but we may communicate in a way that works better to help us connect, rather than disconnect, based on the relationship. Consider having a conversation with your best friend versus having a conversation with your boss. While you are not changing who you are, you are quite likely to structure the conversation differently because of whom they are and how your lives intersect. By adapting our style for each environment, situation, and relationship as we encounter them, we can ensure we have a greater opportunity for effectiveness and mutually beneficial relationships.

Putting It All Together

Remember, DISC is not a measure of intelligence, skills, education, or experience and is not an indicator of values. DISC identifies how behavioral patterns influence what a person wants, needs, and expects of themselves and from others, and how people communicate those wants, needs, and expectations. DISC is only one piece of the puzzle. The next chapter examines understanding what drives behavior—our motivation.

APPLYING ASSESSMENT SCIENCE

DISC Benefits To Individual:
Self-Awareness And Adaptability

- Simple to understand, practical, and easy to apply the model and assessment tools

- Incredibly accurate results

- All about results and relationships; there is something for everyone

- Normalizes our human experience by showing what we do and how we do it when communicating, and evaluating if that works for our situations and relationships

- A comprehensive wealth of information that helps you determine how to be as effective as possible in a variety of circumstances

- Designed to allow intentionality in actions and emotions. Once you are aware, you can choose to do something differently, if necessary

- Helps us to identify and respond appropriately to the behaviors and communication style of others

- Highly validated and researched with proven results

DISC Benefits To Organizations

- Enhances workplace results and relationships by creating common language and understanding of team member and leader behaviors and needs

- Improves human connection and employee communication

- Helps us understand how we are alike and different

- Reduces conflict and increases harmony in the workplace

- Focuses on the value of diversity on teams and at work

- Encourages managing emotions appropriately in the workplace to prevent misunderstanding and derailed work experiences

- Easy to use for continued learning

- Easy to administer and manage assessments

CHAPTER 4

Identifying And Exploring Motivational Styles: Motivators Assessment

R esearch shows successful people share a common trait of self-awareness and find ways of achieving objectives that align with their core motivations and ultimately, with their goals or purpose. They understand their limitations and can actively identify those situations in which they are not likely to be as effective. Additionally, they can anticipate what will or will not inspire them or motivate them. Furthermore, those who understand their natural motivations are far more likely to pursue the right opportunities for the right reasons and get the results they desire.

While creating a solid understanding of human behavior and emotion through DISC provides a foundation of self-awareness, understanding what makes people tick has other facets.

What if we could understand the core values and motivational drivers of those around us? If we knew what was most important to those we interact with, how might we be able to reduce tension and create better outcomes?

By building a comprehensive knowledge of our own preferences, drivers, and motivations to determine how to effectively reach for satisfaction and success, we can begin to see how to maximize performance by achieving stronger alignment between our motivators, choices, and actions. Then, by building a greater understanding of the motivator dimensions in general, it becomes easier to see how the motivator dimensions influence and guide others' behaviors to move them forward or keep them still.

MOTIVATORS CONCERNS AND RESOLUTIONS

- **Motivators is not 100% accurate.**
  People are complex and can't be described with just one assessment. There may be tendencies that don't fit 100% because humans are multi-faceted and we can't always capture every detail in a short report.

- **Motivators only looks at the values that drive our decisions and actions.**
  That's right, and when used in combination with other tools, we can see how those values influence our decisions and behaviors.

- **Motivators doesn't cover critical thinking in detail.**
  Motivators doesn't fully examine critical thinking skills and decision-making, but provides an opportunity for those things to be explored based on our values and what we determine to be most important.

- **This is a stereotyping tool.**
  Motivators is not meant to be a model to put people in a box and stereotype them. We are all uniquely blended in our Motivators, so this tool allows us insight to help us learn to communicate and interact more effectively.

- **Once I understand Motivators, that's all I need to know.**
  Making assumptions or judgments is never appropriate based on any model, and particularly without fully understanding the nuances of what each dimension represents. These measures act as a starting point for exploration, discussion, and connection and are intended as a resource to help us connect with others and learn about what drives us to be alike and different.

- **Motivators is only a self-perception activity.**
  While it's only one perspective, it can be used to create conversation with others to explore the effects of our own understanding versus their understanding, and to confirm our intentions match others' perceptions.

Understanding Motivators

Motivators are the reasons we want to act. They help us better understand our value hierarchy or belief system. They filter and guide our decisions specifically toward the results that reflect them, and combine uniquely for each of us to influence priorities and decision-making.

Motivators reveal our viewpoint, our mindset, and our paradigm of thought. We all have our own desires, and ideally, we all express those values and desires through our behavior. Our viewpoint or mindset may not be like anyone else. The paradigm we operate from may be different. Understanding what we each value and hold as important can reveal great insights into what will move us or keep us still.

You can also think of it like this: when we value something, we'll only be satisfied when the value is fulfilled. For example, if we value information, we only feel satisfied when we are well-informed. The same thing is true for all our motivational drivers and core values. Understanding our motivators reveals why we would choose to do what we do in certain ways. We are driven by what we want and what we think is important.

There is a catch, though, that is extremely important to recognize:

> *Behavior overrides motivations. While our motivators influ-
> ence and guide us,* **we may act differently than we want to**
> *for a variety of reasons.*

We may have a core value or motivator that does not come out in our behavior. The situation, environment, or relationship may not be supportive of that motivator being expressed. It doesn't mean the motivator isn't important or present; it simply means under these circumstances, that motivator is not satisfied. We may have to find other ways to satisfy that motivator for it to be expressed in a way that is meaningful for us.

For example, maybe our work environment is not as supportive of our value for autonomy and independence. Rather than find a different job, we may be able to satisfy that motivator outside of work instead. When motivators align with our behavior, we have personal synergy. When they don't align, it can create personal conflict and tension. When we understand what drives us, we can be intentional with doing what's necessary to satisfy our motivators.

Understanding Each Other Fully Is The Key To Connection

Consider this scenario:

Hamish and Jayne have been in partnership for a long time. Not only are they happily married, but they own a company they both put all their effort and energy into and are extremely devoted to the success of the venture. They both want their company to be successful, work long hours, and are committed to doing what is best for the business.

Jayne is the client specialist. She is the face of the business, networking and promoting their products endlessly to help bring in more customers and providing excellent service. She values connection, doing what is right and best for her clients, and tries to maintain work-life balance, though that is often difficult because she is so busy.

Hamish is the man behind the curtain, constantly striving to keep the company organized, the employees engaged and productive, and making sure things run smoothly. He wants everything to be right and practical, and wants to see results that clearly benefit the company and his family.

With different roles, you can anticipate they might have different adapted behavioral styles as well to help them be effective at work. With different motivators, Jayne and Hamish are likely focusing on different things that are important to them which could create misunderstanding and challenges if they don't recognize what each other values.

Remember, learning to understand each other is the key to successful connection.

To help us learn more about one another, the Motivators assessment report tool offers an in-depth identification and exploration of seven Motivators Dimensions: *Aesthetic, Economic, Individualistic, Power, Altruistic, Regulatory,* and *Theoretical.*

Keep in mind, the scores in each determine how strong that Motivator is, both how important it is to you and how you value it.

While it's helpful to explore each motivator and what it means individually, it is *critical* to remember these cannot be completely separated. Each interacts with the others to create our motivational drivers, so they must be interpreted *together* for the greatest accuracy and to evaluate the strength or influence of the Motivators on our decisions and actions. All seven must be evaluated and examined together to see how they are affecting and influencing one another.

The report graphs reveal your own Motivators based on what is important to you right now and show what your values and beliefs look like compared to the other dimensions. You'll see a comprehensive view of how your Motivators compare to the population. You may be more like the population, or you may value the dimensions differently, and that insight can bring further clarity to your own drive and values and how they interact with what others believe and value.

Furthermore, the Motivators assessment offered by Assessments 24x7 outlines a series of resources and reflection opportunities to apply your new knowledge immediately. With this tool, you can easily deepen your understanding of self, bring awareness to what drives you to do what you do, and provide greater insight to those around you to create even better connections.

The History Of Motivators

In 1914, German philosopher and psychologist Eduard Spranger published a book in German titled *Lebensformen* (later translated into English in 1928 as *Types of Men: The Psychology and Ethics of Personality*). In it, he described the research and observations that led to identifying six attitudes, values, or motivators he found present in every person. These six values were what he believed created motivation and drive in an individual, and he defined them as, "world views or filters that shape and define that which a person finds valuable, important, good, or desirous."

Values are formed through repeated experiences and multiple exposures to the world. Your experiences help determine your attitude or beliefs about what is valuable or good and what is not. The more positive the encounters associated with any dimension, the more reinforced that dimension becomes as being valuable and good. Conversely, the more negative the encounters, the less reinforced the dimension becomes. Due to their connection with experiences and environment, our values are dynamic. With enough time or experience, an individual's value hierarchy can change. It is, however, very slow to change outside of a significant emotional event or crisis. Therefore, it is very important that people understand their motivators and drivers since they are primarily static.

The original six dimensions were:

- Aesthetic—The aesthetic person sees highest value in form and harmony.

- Economic—The economic person is characteristically interested in what is useful.

- Political—The political person is interested primarily in power and control.

- Social—The highest value for a social type is love of people.

- Religious—The highest value of the religious may be called unity.

- Theoretical—The dominant interest of the theoretical person is the discovery of truth.

In the 1950's, American psychologist Gordon Allport picked up where Spranger left off and became one of the first psychologists to really focus on personality in the United States. He rejected both Freud's psychoanalytic approach to personality, which he thought went too deep, and Marston's behavioral approach, which he thought did not go deep enough. He placed the most importance on the uniqueness of each individual, and the importance of the present context, as opposed to past history, for understanding the personality. Allport believed people's personalities are largely founded upon their values or basic convictions they hold about what is and is not of real importance in life. From this assumption, he began to outline the major value types.

Working from Spranger's model, Allport and his partner Philip Vernon, created the first values instrument to allow for measuring a person's values hierarchy, the Allport & Vernon Study of Values, in 1931. The work was revised in 1970 and Gardner Lindzey's name was added. Since its publication, it is the third-most-cited nonprojective personality measure. By 1980 the use of the instrument was declining primarily because of dated language and cultural changes. Richard Kopelman, et.al., updated the instrument in 2003, and the copyrighted version was published in Elsevier Science. Permission is required for current use.

The first computerized values instrument was authored in 1985-87 by Russell Watson, a psychology professor. Watson discovered some nuances within the Political theme that encouraged him to explore and define the Individualistic dimension. This dimension expanded the creative, unique, and out-of-box thinking drive as opposed to a drive for power, control, and influence as in the Political theme. The instrument was called the Business Values Inventory, and published in 1988 by another assessment company. Watson chose to use six values themes, dropping the Aesthetic theme and inserting the Individualistic theme. The reason for dropping the Aesthetic theme was that in thousands of samples, the Aesthetic score was consistently ranked as the lowest theme. Current versions of values assessments will include five, six, and seven themes. The current work by Assessments 24x7 includes Allport's original six themes, and adds Watson's Individualistic dimension.

Nature Versus Nurture

Spranger championed nature (genetics) as having the greatest influence on our value hierarchy. He wrote, "Become what you are," which could be interpreted to mean, "Become aware of what motivates you, what you value, what inspires you—and be true to it."

Allport, on the other hand, championed nurture (socioeconomic influences of childhood) as being of greater influence on our value system. Most modern researchers today favor something in the middle—a mix of nature and nurture that finds a genetic predisposition to certain traits, tendencies, talents, and abilities that must be activated through exposure to certain environmental conditions. It's like having a genetic predisposition to diabetes, but not everyone with those genetic markers contracts the disease. It takes exposure to certain conditions like poor diet, obesity, or illness to bring on diabetes.

So, while our values definitely change and grow, they do so over the course of our lives, not rapidly over a weekend. In other words, they are pretty much fixed for longer periods of time. Therefore, it's important to understand them, so they can be optimally aligned with what, or more accurately, why we do the things we do. For example, if I'm predominantly motivated by altruism (helping others at the expense of self), yet my job motivates me most significantly by economic (a return on investment) means, I won't find nearly as much passion and reward in what I do. While the monetary incentive may be great, it doesn't necessarily mean I am helping others the way I wish I could, for example.

Understanding what drives you, what motivates you, what inspires you, and what is deemed important by you is a vital first step in improving performance, satisfaction, and happiness in life.

The Evolution Of The Motivator Assessment Tool

The motivational instrument now has seven dimensions instead of six. Along with retaining both dimension changes already discussed, the new tool also replaces Spranger's original Religious with the Regulatory dimension. Unlike the substitution of Individualistic for Political, this is not a replacement, rather a name and instrument change. To comply with contemporary Equal Employment Opportunity Commission (EEOC) demands, it is not appropriate to have a profile that asks specific questions about religious preferences, nor is it really an accurate representation of what the dimension is comprehensively about anyway. The new profile uses Regulatory in place of the older Religious title and removes any mention of religious preference in the instrument itself.

Understanding The Motivators Dimensions

With the evolution complete, the seven Motivators dimensions are:

- **Aesthetic** (original)—drive for balance, harmony, and form

- **Economic** (original)—drive for return on investment

- **Individualistic** (Allport)—drive to stand out as independent and unique

- **Power** (Spranger Political)—drive to be in control or have influence

- **Altruistic** (Spranger Social)—drive to help others at the expense of self

- **Regulatory** (Spranger Religious)—drive to establish order, routine, and structure

- **Theoretical** (original)—drive for knowledge, learning, and understanding

Based on Drs. Spranger and Allport, here are expanded definitions for each dimension:

Aesthetic: High Aesthetic people see the highest value in form, balance, and harmony. Each experience is judged from the standpoint of grace, symmetry, or fit. These people regard life as a procession of events; each event is enjoyed and examined for how it brings about emotion or aligns with what is most important to them, with an emphasis on self-expression. They need not be a creative artist, or decadent, but have a chief interest in the beauty and harmony of life.

High Aesthetic individuals will not be concerned with the practical, real-world approach, but instead look for what's pleasing, intriguing, and beautiful. The high Aesthetic style is not concerned with the functionality of things; it is more important that things be attractive and interesting. Originality is key. Those who score high in this dimension are often described as eccentric and unconventional, having an alternative perspective that many would consider outside-the-box thinking.

Alternatively, low Aesthetic people find value in the practical, realistic, and sensible. For this style, function is everything; if it does what is intended and makes sense, that is what matters. This pragmatism carries into all areas of life, so harmony and balance, unless useful and sensible, may not be valued. Low Aesthetic people will be seen as having their feet on the ground rather than their head in the clouds.

Economic: High Economic people are characteristically interested in what is useful and beneficial to them. Based originally upon the satisfaction of bodily needs (self-preservation), this type is focused on the return on investment, whether that be time, attention, money, service, etc. The return can be as different as the individual, but there must usually be something in it for them. High Economic people are thoroughly practical and conform well to the prevailing stereotype of a businessperson because of the drive for competition and winning. Highly Economic people want education to be practical and applicable for the greatest return now, and regard unapplied knowledge as a waste. The high Economic style is often perceived as self-interested, or even selfish, because of the high demand for the practical and receiving incentives equal to the output.

Alternatively, low Economic individuals find value in doing and being for others. While they are often perceived as aloof and reserved, they are simply not connected to self-interest, and will frequently focus on what they can do to help others get what they want, rather than going for their own goals or dreams. Low Economic styles are frequently seen settling for what they can get, rather than fighting for what they want. The motto for a high Economic style may be "what's in this for me?" but those with a low Economic style are more worried about how everyone will benefit and less concerned with what will come to them as a result.

Individualistic: High Individualistic people seek to be separate and independent. Their desire is to stand out, to express their uniqueness, and be granted freedom and autonomy over their own actions. Innovation is the driver. They are likely to do and say things that will earn external attention or validation, not for the sake of self-expression, but for the sake of being noticed as distinctive. This is an interesting dimension specifically because while high Individualistic people want to be unique and different, they do not want to be so unusual that they are alienated from the community. The idea is to be noticed, not to be an outcast. Often, the high Individualistic style will be perceived as needing to have the last word, saying unusual things to cause others to stop and take note, and searching for a way to be in the spotlight.

Alternatively, low Individualistic people may disappear into the background, preferring anonymity to acknowledgement. They will not seek attention or validation and are seen to be more secure with themselves, as they don't need someone else to recognize or make a fuss over them. Low Individualistic styles tend to be far more supportive and accommodating to others and are often seen as collaborative and caring team players. Stability and security are priorities.

Power: High Power people are interested primarily in authority, influence, and control. Their activities are not necessarily within the field of politics or leadership, but whatever their vocation, they may portray themselves as authoritative and controlling, seeming heartless and harsh in order to maintain that power. This can be either effective or ineffective. Leaders in any field generally have high power and control values as they desire to drive the action and have influence over the environment and outcome. Since competition and struggle play a large part in all life, many philosophers have seen power as the most universal and fundamental of motives. There are those who wish above all else for personal power, influence, and renown.

Those low in Power are much more likely to yield their position for the sake of allowing others to lead. These styles are more inclined to thrive through supporting others rather than enjoying taking the reins, particularly if there is opportunity for conflict or controversy. Low Power styles will gladly allow others to lead the charge and move the masses in the necessary direction.

Altruistic: The highest value for Altruistic people is the desire to sacrifice themselves for the good of others. High Altruistic people prize other people, often more than themselves, and are kind, sympathetic, and unselfish. In many cases, for those very high in this dimension, there is also often a self-worth challenge that drives the external focus on others. These individuals will do and be for others in an attempt to "earn their keep" or prove their value and worth through doing for others.

Often, this dimension is misrepresented by an assumption that high Altruistic means individuals like people, and low Altruistic is a dislike of people. That is not true, though low Altruistic people are often characterized as being skeptical of the intentions of others and more self-focused. Low Altruistic has a higher level of discernment of where, to whom, and how to apply energy. People who are low Altruistic will look at others to determine if they deserve help or support and if investing that energy is worth it. Once a person is determined to be deserving, low Altruistic styles can be very helpful and supportive and quite generous, particularly when that generosity also works for their betterment.

Regulatory: High Regulatory people understand and shape their interactions with the world through clear boundaries, standards, regulations, and rules. Regulatory people are those whose mental attitude is directed toward achieving structure and are focused on satisfying this value through order and a narrow constitution. Some of this type find life's value in the affirmation of systems or processes and in active participation in it. "Traditionalists" seek to unite with a higher order—to be one with the system. Often, this system is built of a strong commitment to a belief system, defined by individuals as right, regardless if others may agree. Proud of a very concrete, right-and-wrong mindset, these styles are sure there is a best way, and usually only one way, to get things done and solve problems.

A low Regulatory value indicates a strong desire for flexibility, options, independence, and even pushing back against the rules and standards. Often, those low in this dimension seem defiant, especially to those who are higher in the dimension, because they believe there is not necessarily only one way to get things done or solve a problem. They are resistant to structure, regulations, boundaries, and standards, and prefer a much less restrictive mindset.

Theoretical: The dominant interest of High Theoretical people is the discovery of truth, uncovering as much information as possible to become the ultimate expert. In the pursuit of this goal, they characteristically take a cognitive attitude, one that looks for identities and differences. They seek to observe, reason, and understand every element and how it operates and influences the things it touches. Since the interests of the Theoretical are empirical, critical, and rational, they are typically intellectualists, preferring to examine everything as a scientist or philosopher to gain, order, and systematize knowledge. Driven by an authentic curiosity, this style will make every effort toward learning and discovering more, just for the sake of learning.

A low Theoretical style is far less driven by the desire for truth or discovery of information. Instead, this style looks for the most relevant information that is immediately applicable, and may not retain it for a moment more than they deem useful. Often seen as disinterested, this style relies on what they already know, coupled with what feels right through intuition and instinct, and if that doesn't work, they'll try something else. They frequently do not retain information, and are often experimenting through trial and error in their learning and application. Typically, they only need just enough information to be successful and effective within their circumstances, and are quick to move on to something else as they see fit, rather than commit to learning all they can about a particular subject or interest.

More About Each Style

The chart below, created in partnership with Steven Sisler & Behavioral Resource Group, will help you understand the characteristics of each of the styles, based on a short descriptor from low scoring to high scoring. It is easy to see that the characteristics of someone high in a style are contrary, or opposite, to someone low in that motivator dimension. Just like DISC, Motivators are bi-axial (or polarized); the high style characteristics are the opposite of low style characteristics.

Eccentric	Self-Mastered	Unrestricted	Domineering	Subservient	Black and White	Scholarly
Impractical	Maximized	Independent	Forceful	Sacrificial	Fixed	Fact-Finder
Unconventional	Competitive	Self-Reliant	Authoritative	Accommodating	Systemic	Studious
Divergent	Incentivized	Creative	Controlling	Obliging	Orderly	Investigative
Imaginative	Practical	Balanced	Directive	Supportive	Disciplined	Inquisitive
Sensible	Judicious	Cooperative	Influential	Helpful	Open-Minded	Reflective
Realistic	Relaxed	Accommodating	Supportive	Self-Protective	Flexible	Street Smart
Practical	Aloof	Supportive	Yielding	Suspicious	Independent	Intuitive
Real World	Apathetic	Apprehensive	Passive	Distrusting	Spontaneous	Surface Analyzer
Grounded	Satisfied	Secure	Submissive	Self-Focused	Defiant	Disinterested
AES	ECO	IND	POW	ALT	REG	THE

Intensities Of Motivator Styles

As with DISC, Motivators operates on a scale of intensity, however DISC intensities are measured as a number scale typically (in the case of Assessments 24x7's report, the scale is shared in two ways: 1 to 6 and 1 to 100), whereas Motivators is a scale of qualified descriptors: very low, low, average, high, and very high. These ranges are used to group characteristics that are similar for people scoring within that particular range. Remember, as with DISC, very low and very high are characterized with descriptors that are opposites of each other.

Also, just like DISC, there are some special intensity circumstances that are helpful to understand. An important note to the intensity of Motivator styles is in the very high and very low scores; there are both *overextended* and *underextended* scores noted in the dimensions. One difference in Motivators is that the numbers that indicate an over or underextended score are not necessarily 90 and 10, respectively. Each dimension of Motivators has its own range of over and under extensions. In either case, whether very high or very low, these scores have a specific connection to the Motivators style just like they do with DISC—the desires associated *become a need versus a want*. When Motivators become extreme, either high or low, people will create an environment where those Motivator needs can be satisfied. Their behaviors and drivers must be fulfilled to relieve brain tension. If the score is over or underextended, the tension must be resolved, so the Motivator must be satisfied.

It is essential to recognize the intense scores (low and high) for what they are: a requirement, a need. By building awareness of what drives the behaviors associated with the intensities, we can learn how to best create an environment that supports us and to have an understanding of what others need as well.

Furthermore, it is important to note the significance of average scores. Average scores are indicators of a score near the middle of the range, and like most everyone else (or the norm). For scores that measure as average, this indicates a situational approach to the Motivator. Another way to think about it is that it depends. Sometimes one Motivator may be more important, and sometimes it may be less important; we will decide depending on the situation. If the scores are average and near the center, there is not a passion toward or away from that Motivator that will be noticeable. If we don't have a connected passion, we are neither driven to nor away from action in that Motivator. Generally speaking, it is uncommon for someone to have completely balanced or flat scores, where all areas are within average or near the center. In fact, if this is the case, that is often an indicator of a potential concern, as that person would appear passionless, with no particular drive or pull in any Motivator. More commonly, most people have clear areas of passion that stand out as higher or lower.

Shifting Styles

Motivators are created in us as a combination of nature and nurture, what we are born with and what we learn as we grow. For most, Motivators are fairly solidified and hardwired in us by the time we reach adulthood. However, that is not to say our Motivators cannot change temporarily. Motivators reflect what is most important to us which can be changed with effort and energy.

Consider the story of a client partner, Juan. Juan had operated his entire existence as a high Altruistic, low Economic. He was more concerned with helping and doing for others than for himself, until it came time for Juan to consider retirement. At sixty-three, Juan knew he was not far from the target age that would allow him to move into the next phase of his life. But Juan had spent his working life helping others, sacrificing for the greater good, and had inadequately prepared himself for life without a steady income. Over the course of the next two years, Juan found himself with a great deal of urgency around needing retirement income and a plan for his impending freedom. In every interaction, Juan decided to very intentionally ask himself if it was worth his attention, time, and resources, and to be incredibly diligent about ensuring a return on any investment with which he engaged. By actively seeking to bring about a new return on his investment, Juan effectively raised his Economic score and lowered his Altruistic score. This took a great deal of attention and a committed effort, but when he reassessed, his scores had indeed shifted. It should be noted that once Juan felt prepared for retirement, and that level of return on investment and self-interest was no longer as urgent, Juan's scores returned much closer to his previous measured importance. While Juan's focus of importance temporarily shifted, his hardwired, instinctual Motivators didn't actually change permanently. He was still high Altruistic, low Economic Juan who had a different commitment for a while.

Putting It All Together

As previously stated, Motivators are not meant to be used as seven standalone measures, nor are they intended to be used as an exclusive model without examining how they interact with a person's DISC style blend (and other assessment data, if possible). The power of understanding Motivators comes first in identifying how each dimension operates, but then connecting them all together for a comprehensive view, a holistic perspective of what drives behaviors. In an ideal world, once we know what motivates an individual, the DISC styles will align to create synergy. This is not always the case, however; there are times when our Motivators and DISC do not align and can be indicative of tension, rather than synergy.

To put it simply, we can't always do what we wish we could—for a variety of reasons.

DISC identifies how behavioral patterns influence what a person wants, needs, and expects from you and others and how people communicate those. With Motivators as a part of the equation, we get a deeper look at why we do what we do, by peeling back another layer of what makes us tick and applying that to our own self-understanding and relationships with others. DISC and Motivators are a powerful combination.

APPLYING ASSESSMENT SCIENCE

Motivators Benefits To Individual: Self-Awareness And Adaptability

- Simple to understand, practical, and easy to apply the model and assessment tools

- Incredibly accurate results

- Normalizes our human experience by showing why we do what we do and how that relates to others' drivers and values

- A comprehensive wealth of information that helps you determine how to be as effective as possible in a variety of circumstances by understanding your own desires and how to connect to others' desires

- Designed to allow intentionality in actions and emotions; once you are aware, you can choose to do something differently, if necessary

- Helps us to identify and respond appropriately to the wants, needs, and behaviors of others

- Highly validated and researched with proven results

Motivators Benefits To Organizations

- Enhances workplace results and relationships by creating common language and understanding of team member and leader needs and wants

- Improves employee connection

- Helps us understand how we are alike and different

- Reduces conflict and increases harmony in the workplace

- Focuses on the value of diversity on teams and at work

- Easy to use for continued learning and development

- Easy to administer and manage assessments

Assessments In Action: DISC and Motivators

E ach of the assessments highlights specific areas that help us to learn more about our individual approach to the world, and provide the opportunity to be intentional with our behaviors, needs, wants, interactions, choices, decisions, and actions. As you review the following case studies and examples, be mindful that these are specific to DISC and Motivators and do not take into consideration Emotional Intelligence or Critical Thinking.

DISC Case Study 1

The Situation

A manager approaches a trainer after a workshop to ask for some support with his general manager. The general manager has not taken an assessment.

They work together closely and frequently, but the manager is frustrated by an inability to have successful interactions with the general manager (GM).

- The GM shows the need to assert himself in a room or make his presence known. He seems to want people to look up to him and admire him.

- The GM constantly interrupts or chimes in with a new task or joke when not necessarily appropriate (maybe to bring the attention back to him).

- The GM seems to need to control conversations, not guide those involved or allow conversations to happen organically.

- The manager describes the GM as being a Type A personality, someone with an intense, sustained drive to achieve goals, an eagerness to get things done, and a persistent desire for recognition and advancement who is quick, mentally alert, and a super-achiever.

The Questions

What style do you think he is, even though he hasn't taken the assessment? What would you recommend regarding positive interactions? What can be done to ensure the GM is not negatively affecting the team and those important clients around him? What strategies can others use with him to communicate as effectively as possible?

The Observations And Insights

Without seeing his assessment scores, we can only use what we observe in his behavior and emotions. It is very likely the GM is both a high D and I. The high D would show up in the need for control, and the high I manifests in the need for attention, to be admired, and the way in which he draws attention to himself.

It's quite possible he is overextended (with very high scores) in both, and if so, he has a behavioral *need* associated with each, which is different from a behavioral tendency. For the D, the need is to win and dominate—we call this the "warrior spirit," fighting for survival and being the best no matter what. Overextended I styles have a need for control and connections, and maintain that control by keeping people close and often overpersuading, which can feel like manipulation to others. If this is the case, it will be important to be aware of the potential need for control over people as well as results.

This style can indeed be a challenge for others to communicate with sometimes and the key is self-awareness. If he does not have high emotional intelligence, he may not be aware of how his behavior impacts others and can be perceived negatively and counterproductive in relationships. He will have a fear of losing social acceptance as well as control, so if he understands how his behavior can potentially cause both of those things to become reality, that might be an eye-opener.

The Strategies

If he is behaving as a high D and/or high I, shutting him out or keeping him out of processes altogether, especially if he was previously involved, may push his buttons. He would feel like he has no control and is losing social acceptance. Instead, a more appropriate response may be to use "freedom with fences." He needs clear boundaries. If it's possible to allow him to be involved with boundaries, or ask for his input in a way that won't be disruptive to the team, that could help. For example, ask for input via email instead of in a meeting.

If he's to be involved in a meeting, before discussing a topic, set a clear expectation. For example, "Okay, team. We need to discuss XX. I want to make sure this is as comfortable and respectful environment as possible so I can hear your good thoughts. I value your input, so I really want this to be a time to listen to each other. Also, I want to make sure we can hear from everyone who wants to contribute, so be mindful of the time we have. Can we all agree to that?"

That way, it doesn't call him out publicly, and he knows the expectation. If he is still disruptive in meetings, it might be a good idea to get his input via email.

Keep in mind, the style of the manager can also be a factor. If the manager is a high S or C and doesn't like confrontation, that could actually be enabling the situation. If the manager is also a high D or I, he/she could be volleying and pushing for who can have the most power and attention.

The bottom line is that interacting and being a part of the team is fine, as long as it's not disruptive and counterproductive. The GM will likely need to directly be told where the line is, but this should happen in private. If done publicly, he may get angry. His high I will feel the sting of public social embarrassment, so the high D in him will fight for survival and lash out to save face.

Anytime we are "managing up" or managing our manager, the communication can be difficult. Once we understand our own style strengths and limitations and have awareness of their needs, fears, and emotions, we can more effectively ensure that our interactions build and maintain mutually-beneficial relationships.

DISC Case Study 2

The Situation

A small team that works closely together has a peer supervisor who seems difficult. She's nice enough most of the time, but there are constant challenges with the team not wanting to work with her. People talk in the break room about how she'll be at work that day. "Will we see Great Carol or Grumpy Carol?" No one ever really knows what to expect and what might set her off. She does really good work,

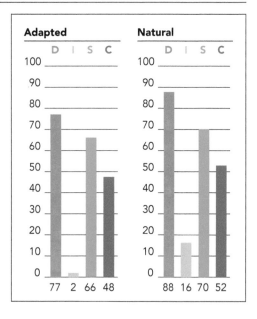

but it seems like sometimes if things don't go her way, she reacts poorly. Sometimes she's interested in being a part of the team, and sometimes she's very critical and demanding with the group.

The Questions

Why does this person shift so quickly and in such drastic ways? What can the team do to be more successful when interacting with Carol? How can team members give her what she needs or wants, when they struggle to figure it out? How do they protect themselves from the emotional back and forth? Should the team just maintain distance and not try to interact?

Observations/Insights

Carol is struggling with two competing and quite different styles (D/S). Some days, she wants things planned out and is very clear in the communication and process steps. Other days, she'll leave information out, allowing actions to be based on assumptions. Sometimes it needs to be done now and close enough is good enough; other times, it should be done right, and everyone should take time to be sure the results are accurate. In one moment, Carol seems to impulsively make a decision and be fine with implementing a change right now, but then she wants to stop and plan it out, and may even disregard the previous plan or result and come up with something completely different. She tells team members they are "here to work smarter, not harder," but the team knows harder is required to be sure things are done well and completely. At one moment, Carol might allow others to work through the process, encouraging input, supporting collaboration and engagement, but at other times, she becomes impatient and direct, taking control, and becoming frustrated when others ask a question or provide feedback.

Because we are seeing opposite styles at play, we are experiencing a push and pull with styles that are different from one another, specifically in Pace, Priority, and expressed tendencies: *Faster/Slower, People/Task, Open/ Guarded and Direct/Indirect.* Consider these comparisons of focus, tendencies, and characteristics:

- The D is task, the S is relationship.

- The D is risk, the S is stability and predictability.

- The D is movement and takes by force, the S is hesitancy and receiving what comes to them.

- The D is driving, the S is hoping.

- The D is aggressive, the S is passive.

- The D is very assertive and the S is very supportive.

- The D is impulsive, the S is cautious.

- The D is doing, the S is helping.

- The D is anger, the S is patience and non-expression.

- The D needs, creates, and accepts challenges while the S needs, creates, and accepts stability.

- The D is demanding, the S is suggesting.

This style often shows up as the dog you don't know if you can pet. They shift so swiftly from one emotion to the other that they are often unpredictable and difficult to read. These styles judge others by achievements and results, according to how they would expect the results to be themselves. If something does not work out the way they think it should, they are easily derailed and may not know how to move forward gracefully; they'll often respond with anger and frustration, which may or may not be expressed depending on how high the S style measures. They tend to be hard-working, resourceful, and determined—often to the point of being workaholics—and likely also feel like what they are working for is the success and support of others.

If emotional intelligence is high, they can recognize their impact on others, and potentially calm, reassure, and support them. It may take a bit of time to get to that perspective, though; they likely respond in anger first, then after taking time to process and deal with the emotions, come back to a logical mindset.

While they are direct and guarded, they are also indirect and open, so any disagreement or conflict may be taken personally. It is important to be sure that coaching is not given in a personal manner, "when you do this X, it results in this Y;" but rather, "the situation X can impact the results Y."

It is also beneficial to note the very low I score in the adapted style. This underextended score (less than 10) represents a behavioral need that must be fulfilled for Carol. The need of underextended I style is to have control by protecting themselves from others (like pushing others away and keeping them at a distance so they cannot get too close). This underextension often is viewed as someone who prefers to work alone, is very detail oriented, prefers a controlled environment, is likely to be pessimistic, and lacks trust. With all the other things we know about the D/S style, this adds another element to what might be happening with Carol and her interactions with others.

The Strategies

Remember, Carol wants control, so options are important. She will be driven by deep emotions and connections, and will need to understand where others are coming from and their values, so she doesn't impose her own values and standards on them. She will seem even more demanding and less connected if she doesn't stop to listen and value what other people are sharing/valuing.

Focus on what happens in stress, especially how she may be perceived by others, to help her understand how she is perceived. Remember, we all operate from some degree of stress and tension, and the D/S combination is often wound tighter than a spring most of the time. Because they are often so close to emotional and behavioral overload, it is imperative they are willing to create awareness of themselves and the impact they have on others.

Are they coachable in this present time or frame of mind? Are they willing to adapt? Do they understand how they are being perceived, and can they take responsibility and do things differently when necessary?

Depending on your own style, this behavior may be more difficult to adjust to or accept. For a high S, the volatility alone may be paralyzing because there is no predictability and the interaction can feel unsafe. The D/S will not likely understand how damaging that can be. A high I may feel personally attacked when the D/S comes through as domineering.

To more effectively create a mutually beneficial relationship, it is essential to communicate with these styles according to their style. Since the D is so prominent, start with how this interaction and your feelings impact their ability to get results. Then, move to how the message would resonate with the S part of their style: how these behaviors impact the team/others. In essence, you will do best to connect with both styles, creating awareness of their fears and needs based on both at the same time.

Interesting Insights: DISC Styles

There are some common situations that often result in questions about the styles. Here are a few interesting DISC style nuances that are beneficial to understand, should you encounter them.

A Low D Style Acts Like A High D

A low D style can act or respond like a high D when their own boundaries or values are pushed or overtaken.

When the other three styles are above the energy line, and therefore expressed at the same time, it creates a heightened level of passion for the things they care about. The emotions, characteristics, needs, and fears of all three styles are in play all at once and are sometimes in conflict with each other, which can cause emotional, pace, and priority tensions.

As a result, if the style boundaries are pushed, it can cause a response that is very much like a high D. For example, if a high S has been patiently awaiting a decision from an authority and cannot move forward with his own job until that happens, he might become very direct, list out the options very clearly, and ask for a final answer now, which is a typical D response (sometimes this is called the "hidden D"). This may take others by surprise, and they might read the emotion as anger. The person may have no idea it is coming across that way; to him, he has simply reached his high threshold for patience in this situation and the combined emotions of optimism/trust/patience/non-expression/fear/concern all at once give the appearance of anger and impatience, the emotions of the D. Whatever the boundary, whatever the style, and whatever the behavioral need or fear that gets triggered, because of the style combination, tensions, and expression, the resulting behavior can resemble that of a high D.

Remember, anger is the primary emotional response for a D, but there is more to anger than just being mad. Anger is not the same as angry—*anger is an urgency and immediate response to invoke action, based on a variety of other emotional drivers*. It can be an expression of frustration, fear, hurt, embarrassment, worry, disappointment, anxiety, shame, and more—all of which can exist in other styles' needs and fears. And the longer the style is in constant tension, the more likely at some point, the person will reach this threshold and push back in a way that may not be as expected.

Styles That Do Not Adapt Their Behavior (Consistency In Natural And Adapted Style)

It does happen that some people will have consistency in their two graphs. While no style is better than any other, and while DISC is not a model of right and wrong when it comes to style, there are some things to be aware of when a person's style stays consistent *despite* the environment, situation, or relationship. There are a few things to explore when you see consistency in graphs:

- Remember, the graphs are a snapshot of a moment in time. It's possible the adapted style is measuring a circumstance where people can express their behaviors in a way that is consistent with their natural style.

- If through the conversation, it is clear people are not adapting their style in this particular situation, exploring why the consistency exists is essential. Return to the three questions to determine if this is the way to go: "Does it make sense?" "Is it necessary?" "Is it effective?" If there is not a reason to shift style, consistency with the natural tendencies is likely a good use of energy.

- If it's clear through the conversation people are not adapting their style in *any* situation, this can present a risk in either awareness or action. It is essential to determine if individuals are not aware they may need to adapt their style to the environment, situation, or relationship, or if they are not able to adjust their style. There are times when individuals simply don't recognize the need to adapt or have an expectation that everyone else will adapt to them. Sometimes, for very high styles, it requires a great deal more energy and effort to adapt to styles that are not like their own. In some cases, people may recognize they could do things differently to be more effective in building mutually beneficial relationships, but they are not able to (or not willing to) put in the energy and effort to actually make the shift. Any of these potential causes of consistency are potentials for risk of ineffectiveness because they limit the ability to engage The Platinum Rule. Once the cause for consistency is determined, it may be necessary to begin to explore and practice what adaptability looks like, and identify ways to effectively recover after adapting.

Opposite Styles Being Expressed (DS, SD, IC, CI)

It is not incredibly uncommon that people will express opposite behavioral styles, and therefore, tendencies and characteristics that seem disconnected from and contradictory to one another. Have you ever met someone who seems to be very fast-paced and expressive and then slows things down and becomes non-expressive at the same time? When you encounter someone who seems to be a walking contradiction, there is a chance this person is pulling from two opposite styles. Not only can this be difficult and confusing for others to respond to effectively, it can be troublesome for the person who may struggle with knowing the best way to proceed with decisions, feeling constantly pulled in two directions. By understanding how and why this behavior exists, you are in a position to be intentional with your behavioral choices, looking for the most effective way to respond to and manage the environment, situation, or relationship by leveraging an understanding of the styles and when they work best.

The Best Leaders And Salespeople (They Aren't Always D Or I Styles)

There is a common misconception out there that the best leaders and salespeople are always D or I styles. This is not always the case. While there are some very helpful characteristics in both the D and I style behaviors and emotions that support successful leadership and sales, there is not a best or worst style for leading or selling. Any style can be a successful leader. Any style can be a successful salesperson. Skills, abilities, experience, passion for the products and service, and individual motivations are essential to understand, too.

Furthermore, when considering the best leaders and the best salespeople, it is imperative to consider more than just their own style. Their customer's or client's style is also a part of the equation, so it is really important to look at adaptability as well. Can they shift their style to meet the needs, fears, and emotions of others effectively?

For example, if you have a team full of C styles, they may need a leader who is more aligned with their style in pace and priority to get effective results. A D style may come on too strong for them, and an I style will likely frustrate them. Similarly, if you have a high D style selling to a high S, the high S may feel overwhelmed, rushed, and pressured. Adapting to the style of others is the key, no matter what style you have a tendency to express.

Adaptability And Authenticity

If you're constantly adapting to others, do you risk losing authenticity? Are you compromising who you are by adjusting your style to others' needs and fears? These are big questions. When adapting to others, the goal is never to change who you are or be something you are not. It may seem like a delicate line, but adaptability, when done correctly, is being considerate of the other person and the dynamics of relationship. It is not manipulative or inauthentic. When adapting, you are not becoming something else; you are simply adjusting your behavior in the short term to improve the relationship and reduce tension.

Just like when you travel to different countries where it's important to recognize the cultural differences and expectations, it's also respectful and important to learn to adapt to the individual styles of others. More than you may realize, happiness, effectiveness, and your future can be affected by how well you get along with others in a variety of circumstances. And how well you get along depends in large measure on your ability to adapt. If you're not a very adaptable person and you respond uniformly to all people and styles, you're not going to have much luck with about three-fourths of the population. You're going to be undermining your own efforts to build relationships by only connecting with a small group of people in a way that works.

Adaptability doesn't just mean mimicking or imitating another person's style. It doesn't mean abandoning your identity and your good sense, or giving up things that are important to you. It does mean adjusting your openness and directness and your pace and priority to make the communication work the best it can based on environment, situation, or relationship. Keep in mind, even as you alter your approach to interact better with others, it's important to maintain your own identity. Someone who is too adaptable risks being seen as wishy-washy or insincere.

Furthermore, an important key to note is that effectively adaptable people meet the other person's needs as well as their own. They know how to negotiate relationships in a way that allows everyone to win. With adaptability, they're practicing the spirit of the Golden Rule but in an even more powerful way: The Platinum Rule—treating others as they want and need to be treated.

Adaptability, in essence, means managing your compatibility, and it is a choice. No one style is more adaptable than another, and how each of us adapts will vary. You can choose to be quite adaptable with one person today and less adaptable with that same individual tomorrow. You can choose to be adaptable in one situation and not adapt in another. In any case, adaptability is an important skill for all people. Understanding others, and knowing how to interact with them for mutual benefit, is the goal.

Motivators Case Study 1

The Situation

Charlie was recently promoted from a successful peer on a team to a project manager. For two years, she had been working in the field with a very flexible schedule and a group of people she really liked and respected. They would even have lunch together at a local diner on Fridays to discuss the things they learned each week and help each other with tough client challenges. The new position seemed perfect for Charlie. She was offered

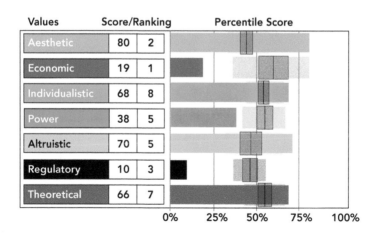

more money, a traditional Monday through Friday, 8 to 5 schedule, and bonuses to do a job she knew she would excel at, one where she could use all her training to advance products and services. However, after just a few months, Charlie is miserable and dreads going to work on Monday. She likes the projects and not having to manage a team, but is unhappy. She knows her new position is a step up, but she just feels like it is not the right job for her, and has confided in her manager that she thinks she made a mistake by taking it. Her manager does not know what to do to help her.

The Questions

What is going on with Charlie? How can her manager help her? Even with the incredible perks the new position offers, why is she struggling to engage in her new role?

Observations/Insights

Using only her Motivators results, it is very easy to see why Charlie is struggling in her new role.

- By looking at Charlie's scores, we can see all her Motivators are outside of the norm scores. She is not driven like others are in most of her Motivators.

- She scores high in Aesthetic, Individualistic, Altruistic, and Theoretical. She scores low in Economic, Power, and Regulatory. The scores show importance: if she values the dimension (high scores are more important to her) and how she values the dimension (how she identifies with the dimension is specific to her score).

- Her ranking shows the impact of those Motivators, with Economic as her most influential and Theoretical as her least impactful.

Charlie's most important Motivators show that for her to be satisfied, she will need to operate in circumstances that allow her:

- An alternative, creative, balanced, and harmonious experience (high Aesthetic)

- The ability to help/support others, with return on investment not needed (low Economic)

- The chance to stand out as unique and special, and to be independent (high Individualistic)

- Minimal authority to lead or manage others, lots of opportunity to contribute to overall team's success (low Power)

- Opportunities to provide support, connection, and help to others (high Altruistic)

- Flexibility, options, and opportunities to try new things (low Regulatory)

- The ability to learn and share important information to help get things done well, in an informed manner (high Theoretical)

Furthermore, when we examine Charlie's motivational patterns, we note:

- Charlie shows a high desire for creativity, innovation, and uniqueness with her high Aesthetic and high Individualistic combination (this can also show up as a passion for something very artistic)

- Charlie has a combination in high Individualistic and low Regulatory that both support her desire for independence and personal freedom

- The combination of high Aesthetic and high Theoretical show Charlie's desire to try new things and have unique and interesting experiences just to know what it's like

- Charlie's low Economic and low Power combination also show that she likely does not desire to be in charge or take the lead,

WHAT MAKES HUMANS TICK?

and will likely be more agreeable and supportive than driving and controlling or competitive

Charlie has moved into a position that does not align well with her Motivators. In her team member position, she had autonomy and flexibility in her schedule, which allowed her work/life balance, the ability to connect with others professionally to learn and create relationships of support, and the opportunity to stand out in her ability to help others with difficult situations. Her values in all seven Motivators were regularly satisfied.

In her new position, she was given more money and a structured schedule, neither of which she really valued. She was also taken from her interactions with others and now works alone developing products and services, which only engage her Theoretical and occasionally Aesthetic Motivators. Sometimes she knows she is helping others with this important project management work, but she rarely sees firsthand how she's contributing or making a difference.

The Strategies

Because so few of her Motivators are being satisfied, it is very likely these disconnects are leading to Charlie's lack of passion in the new role. While the benefits may be many, very little about the position is actually supporting the drivers that are important to her. Charlie and her manager should work together to determine what would be the best and most desirable solution for Charlie.

There are a few options Charlie and her manager could consider:

- Charlie could pursue some new/additional opportunities aligned with her Motivators outside of work. Perhaps her passion can be fulfilled outside of work in a way that still allows her to get what she wants and needs, but in a different environment.

- Charlie and her manager could create opportunities within her role that align with her Motivators. Perhaps Charlie could work an alternative schedule, still have Friday lunches with her old team to connect and catch up, or volunteer on some internal committees that allow her to support her colleagues more.

- Charlie may decide to find a more suitable position that allows her to engage her passions. Perhaps the role really is not the right one for her and she can find something that is a better fit.

Remember, if we were to have a look at her DISC style, we could also see if there are additional concerns from misalignment, or areas of potential synergy and support present that are contributing further to her discontent in her new position. Is she a high I style and misses her interactions with her team? Does she have a high S style and need the opportunity to provide support and stability? The DISC style combined with her Motivators style can make a difference in the interpretation.

Motivators Case Study 2

The Situation

Paul calls his boss to ask for advice on his client, Harry, whose graph is pictured. Paul is struggling because Harry regularly schedules appointments and misses them, reschedules at the last minute, is late for the appointments, or calls over the weekend at unusual hours requesting immediate help from various members on the team, including Paul and the boss. The whole team is frustrated with the client and is starting to feel resentful of Harry's demanding, last-minute approach to everything. More than one team member has talked to Paul about Harry. Harry seems very kind, appreciative, and always complimentary of the service received from Paul's team, but also seems to have no awareness of what comes across as a severe lack of respect and persistent disregard for the schedule or needs of others. Harry's self-centered and urgent requests cause a great deal of stress for Paul and his team, and Paul doesn't know what to do. He wants to continue to work with the client, but at what cost?

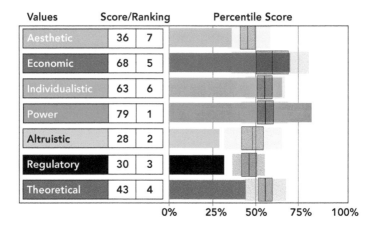

Values	Score/Ranking		Percentile Score
Aesthetic	36	7	
Economic	68	5	
Individualistic	63	6	
Power	79	1	
Altruistic	28	2	
Regulatory	30	3	
Theoretical	43	4	

0% 25% 50% 75% 100%

The Questions

Why does Harry do this? What could be so important at such unconventional times when during work hours appointments are disregarded and missed? How much more should Paul give in to the client to keep him happy and continue to provide good service? How can Paul help the team understand Harry's Motivators so they can all provide the best service they can, and not get frustrated with Harry or Paul?

Observations/Insights

Using only Harry's Motivators graphs, and not taking into consideration his DISC style, we can start to examine what is driving Harry's behavior.

Looking first at the high scores, which note the things that are most important to Harry right now, he values having control and influence (high Power), a return on investment or self-interested benefit (high Economic), and independence, as well as being seen as special and unique high Individualistic).

Examining the rankings, which note the Motivators that will impact Harry's decisions and actions the most (especially if they are aligned with his DISC scores), Harry will be influenced by high Power (control and influence), low Altruistic (self-interest and discernment of return on investment), and low Regulatory (flexibility and independence).

Noting the patterns between scores and rankings, it is easy to see why Harry is behaving in the ways he is. Harry wants what he wants, when he wants it, is focused only on his own needs, and wants to get things done in a way that works for him (which may look like a complete disregard of others, especially if they have different Motivators than he does).

The Strategies

In this case, because of Harry's high Power (desire for control), the combination of high Economic and low Altruistic (self-interest focus), and the combination of high Individualistic and low Regulatory scores (independence and autonomy), communicating with Harry about the impact his actions are having may be difficult. He is not likely to easily see how his actions and decisions are problematic for others, or frankly, may not even care how he is impacting them as long as he gets what he needs or wants. There is a pretty good chance he will do everything in his power to get what he wants when he wants it, despite the effect it has on anyone or anything else.

While frustrating for others, especially those who are different than he is, this does not necessarily mean Harry is a bad person. It simply means he values things differently than others do, and his focus is on his own needs over the needs of others. There can be a real benefit in this approach, but there are obvious limitations, too.

For the sake of Harry, Paul, and Paul's team, the likelihood that Harry's behavior will change is slim. It would benefit Paul and the team more to understand why Harry does what he does, and do their best (within reason, of course) to help Harry as they can. Furthermore, because Harry is likely to continue to behave as he has up to now, the team would do well to set some boundaries to support each other. Perhaps they agree to take turns handling Harry's requests, or send a message to Harry to let him know they will get back to him within 24 hours of any request, but not to expect an immediate response (especially at unusual hours). Alternatively,

Harry could be redirected to Paul again if he tries to work with other team members, so he has only one point of contact to manage the requests.

Remember, sometimes this information is not only helpful in creating and building self-awareness, but helps us to know and understand others. In a case like Harry and Paul, it's less likely Harry will accept that his behavior is challenging for others, and it may be easier for the team to look at how best to adapt to Harry. That does not mean Paul or his team do whatever Harry likes; however, finding a way to work with people, as they are, may be the path of least resistance and most productivity.

Interesting Insights: Motivators

There are some common situations that often spark questions about the dimensions. Here are a few interesting Motivator style nuances that are beneficial to understand, should you encounter them.

Some Motivators Seem In Conflict With One Another

There are Motivators that are contradictory. There is not necessarily a predictable pattern in what we value. We may value things in different ways for different reasons. However, when we see Motivators that are not aligned, it is essential we explore what that means, in which cases that is true, and how that is influencing our behavior and decisions. When we talk about it in coaching and certifications, we talk about tension. If our Motivators are not in alignment with each other, we can experience tension in getting our wants and needs fulfilled.

Consider a graph that shows a high Economic score (a strong desire for return on investment) and a high Altruistic score (a strong desire to help others at the expense of self). By definition, these seem contradictory, and in this case, there could be a strong tension present. How can we want both the greatest benefit to ourselves and to sacrifice for the ultimate benefit of others? Is it about what's best for me, or what's best for you?

However, an alternative could also be true. These two Motivators could align in a way that both can be fulfilled at once, if the return on my investment and what's in it for me is helping others—I am able to do for you and still receive a return on my investment.

The tricky part is knowing if the combination represents synergy or tension. The only way to know is to dive further in, ask questions, and examine how the Motivators play out for each person. No two people are alike, so for one person some combinations may be supportive and for others may cause conflict.

Some Motivators Seem Like they Are Very Similar

There are some Motivators that have very similar characteristics. While there are not always predictable patterns in what we value, as we mentioned previously, there are some interactions between Motivators that create areas of continuity or association that may strengthen one another. Here are a few very common combinations (there are others that are not as common) in Motivators that because they are similar in characteristics, strengthen one another and support each other to bring greater influence to our decisions and actions:

- High Economic and High Power—
  desire for self-benefit and control = competitive

- High Individualistic and Low Regulatory—
  desire for independence and flexibility = autonomy

- High Altruism and Low Economic—
  desire to help benefit others and self-sacrifice = subservient

- High Economic and Low Altruistic—
  desire for self-benefit and suspicion of others = self-interest

- High Aesthetic and High Individualistic—
  desire for creativity and uniqueness = creativity/innovation

The Difference between Importance (Scores) And Impact (Rankings)

This is a tricky concept. The scores and rankings show different measures in Motivators, but both are important.

Remember, scores closer to fifty (or most like the general population) are not noticed as having significant influence in our decisions (because they are more like what everyone else is doing *and* are situational).

- **The score** shows two things: how important the dimension is to you, and how you value it.

  The higher the score, the more important that dimension. (High Aesthetic scores mean being Aesthetic is more important to the person, where a low Economic score means being Economic is not important.) How you value the dimension is revealed by the descriptive characteristic. For example, if I'm very high Aesthetic, "Aesthetic-ness" is important to me, and I express that value as Eccentricity or Impracticality (from the Word Matrix in Motivators).

- **The ranking** shows how influential or impactful this dimension will be on your choices, decisions, and behavior, in order from one as most impactful to seven as least impactful. This does not look at combinations, just at the ranking of the individual dimension. The higher the ranking, the more influence that dimension will be on your decisions and actions.

  For example, if I have a very low Economic score of 14, and Economic ranks as my number one motivator, the score says that being economic (wanting a return on investment) is not important to me—it scores low. The *score* also says I am Apathetic in my Economic dimension, so I'm uninterested and indifferent to getting a return on my investment. The *ranking* says all decisions and actions will be filtered through the low Economic lens; I will almost never look at what's in it for me, but always look at how what I do and don't do impacts others.

Combining DISC And Motivators

While each of the assessments measures something vastly important to the whole person equation, it is the combination that brings the real power of understanding. Let's look at how DISC and Motivators combine to provide greater insight than each report can on its own.

In this example, we'll simply explore what we can see in the graphs as a guideline for interpretation and interaction with the results. Remember, you are always welcome to use the debrief guides online to assist in your interpretation, and we wholeheartedly encourage you to complete the certification programs to learn more.

DISC AND MOTIVATORS EXAMPLE

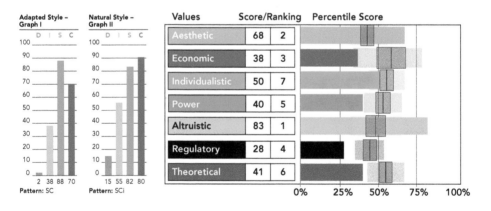

Observations/Insights And Questions

DISC Graph

There is consistency in the natural and adapted style in S, C, and D styles (though there is a slight shift in the scores). The I style shifts significantly from an expressed style in the natural to a concealed style in the adapted. That I shift may cause a great deal of energy use and is worth exploring.

Potential questions to pose to this individual:

Is there a reason for this consistency or shift in style? Does it make sense that your four styles change in the ways they do? Is this shift necessary and effective? How does that energy use with the shifting styles impact you?

There is consistency in pace, for the most part; this person is a slower-paced, more deliberate style. When the I style is engaged, this person may shift to move more quickly in some cases.

Potential questions to pose to this individual:

What are the implications to your effectiveness knowing that you are a slower-paced person? What happens when the faster-paced I style is expressed? What might others think about that shift?

There is an inconsistency in priority; this person focuses both on tasks and people, though the people priority is stronger in both the natural and adapted. Depending on the situation, environment, and relationship, this may be easy to balance, and other times it may feel like this person is being pulled in opposite directions.

Potential questions to pose to this individual:

What are the implications to your effectiveness when your priorities seem to go in different directions? What situations are easy to manage? What situations are difficult to manage? How do you deal with the challenges?

There is consistency in emotions expressed for the most part: non-expression, patience, and fear—and optimism when the I style is expressed/realism or pessimism when it is not.

Potential questions to pose to this individual:

How do these emotions come out? What do others perceive when you have an emotional response, or do not share your emotions? Where do you see your emotions actively or inactively present in your life? What advantages and disadvantages do these emotions have in your experience?

There is one underextended score (adapted D) and one score that is very close to overextended (adapted S). Those over and under extensions represent behavioral needs: D to give in and be agreeable, S to create/maintain safety and stability.

Potential questions to pose to this individual:

How do these behavioral needs show up in your environment, situation, or relationship? Are there times that these are beneficial or detrimental to your effectiveness? What can you do to manage and/or fulfill these needs?

Scores

Based on the Motivators graph, this individual has the following motivational *wants* (Low, Average or High scores) or *needs* (Very High and Very Low scores).

- **Aesthetic**—*Very High: You tend to think alternatively and will likely seek personal fulfillment, creative alternatives, and peace of mind rather than the practical and functional.*

- **Economic**—*Low: You are not driven by monetary rewards or being first and may lack the emotional initiative necessary to compete with those around you.*

- **Individualistic**—*Average: You can both lead and follow and can be flexible between taking a stand or sitting quietly.*

- **Power**—*Low: You are a better collaborator and won't likely seek positions of power or authoritative roles.*

- **Altruistic**—*Very High: You will seek to benefit others at your own personal expense and may find it very difficult to fight for what you want.*

- **Regulatory**—*Very Low: You may subvert or break the rules you feel don't apply and believe in multithreaded approaches to solving problems.*

- **Theoretical**—*Very Low: You are more apt to rely on past experiences and intuition when making decisions.*

Rankings

Very High Altruistic (1), Very High Aesthetic (2) Low Economic (3), Very Low Regulatory (4): *Your decisions and actions will be filtered through (1) what benefits everyone else at your own expense, (2) what is creative, interesting, unusual, feels good, (3) what contributes to everyone else with no required benefit to you, (4) what offers flexibility and lots of options.* (This process can be continued for all seven in order, but we only share four rankings for this demonstration.)

The Combination Of DISC And Motivators

- There is consistency and alignment in your low D, low Economic, and low Power scores; your high S, low Economic and high Altruism score; and your midrange I, midrange Individualistic, and high Aesthetic score.

- There is potential tension in your high C, low Regulatory, and low Theoretical scores, depending on how they interact. Remember—behavior overrides motivation, so you may behave in ways that don't satisfy what you want. If you are looking for additional data and information to support your intuition and past experiences, there will be alignment; however, you may find yourself stuck in a frustrating cycle of wanting more time and information to be sure you are correct (out of fear of doing things wrong—high C) and not satisfying your desire for flexibility and relying on your intuition (low Regulatory and low Theoretical). You will find you often struggle to trust your gut unless you can prove it somehow.

• Overall, there is a lot of consistency and opportunity for your Motivators to be satisfied in your DISC style. Watch for those areas that don't feel right or take a great deal of energy. Remember, you must first put on your oxygen mask before helping others, as they say in the airline industry. You have a tendency to overwhelm yourself and overcommit, and you can't be of use to anyone else if you are not taking care of yourself.

Interesting Insights: DISC And Motivators Combinations

There are some common situations that often result in questions about the combinations of DISC and Motivators. Here are a few interesting nuances that are beneficial to understand, should you encounter them.

Motivators And DISC Style Are Not Aligned Or Motivators Aren't Expressed In DISC Style

Motivators and DISC styles are not always in alignment. As in our previous example, it is possible to have Motivators that do not align with our DISC style. Remember, DISC is our behavior and emotion, and Motivators is what drives those behaviors and emotions—in an ideal sense. But sometimes we are unable to act upon our Motivators; for a variety of reasons, we may not be able to do what we wish we could.

Consider the example of two high Economic and high Power individuals in a relationship. While these same values could create a foundation of understanding and similarity for the partnership, because both high Economic and high Power motivators cause competitiveness, desire for control, and self-interest, if each person operates from that same mindset and seeks to satisfy his/her motivators, the relationship will likely be difficult and adversarial. There is likely to be confrontation, arguments, and opposition to one another, particularly if they are not aligned in a particular belief or circumstance. In this case, to preserve the relationship and make things work, one person is likely to adapt to the other and, in essence, put away his/her motivational wants temporarily for the sake of maintaining the relationship. Ideally, both people toggle in satisfying Motivators to bring balanced satisfaction (i.e., mine is fulfilled this time, yours is fulfilled next time). However, if one person is constantly going with unsatisfied Motivators, the result will be tension for both the person with the restricted Motivators and the relationship.

It is critical to remember that in all cases, behavior will override motivation. We may be a very high Economic Motivator style, but if our behavior is that of a very high S, no one would ever know what motivates us. Our motivation is hidden behind our expression. Behavior will always eclipse motivation when they are not aligned.

A Checklist For Applying The DISC And Motivators Assessments

We certainly don't expect you to be an expert in assessments, but we've provided you with enough information about two of them—DISC and Motivators—to make them part of your assessment process. Here's a checklist you can use to guide your application.

DISC

▶ Review the assessments for key insights and takeaways.

- Examine the graphs for style shifts from natural to adapted.

- Look at differences in pace and priority.

- Explore the emotions expressed in natural and adapted style.

- Evaluate any over or under extensions in scores.

- Look at how you respond to stress and how others perceive that response to ensure your behavior matches your intentions.

- Review the twelve Behavioral Tendencies and look at areas where either you are the outlier or you may be part of a team that doesn't fit the population tendencies.

▶ Have conversations. Don't make assumptions; ask questions.

- When interacting with others, be careful not to put them in a behavioral box. All D styles do not act the same. Instead, look for the needs, fears, and emotions being revealed in the behaviors.

- Ask others about their experiences in various environments, situations, or relationships to understand more about how behavioral expression shows up for them when they adapt. Pay attention to the key circumstances that may impact your relationship.

- Look through the lens of simple, practical, and applicable by asking questions to get to the root of how behavior is being expressed: What am I personally experiencing? What am I seeing in others? How does my behavior and emotion affect others? How am I responding to their behavior and emotion?

▶ Find opportunities for practice and application.

- Use all conversations to practice identifying styles by observable descriptors, behavioral and emotional triggers, and watching for style shifts.

- Be authentically open and curious to learn about others to employ The Platinum Rule—treating others the way they want and need to be treated.

- Continue to be diligent in identifying styles during interactions. That person who was behaving as a high I yesterday may be responding differently today. It's likely not personal, but rather situational.

- Consider advantages and disadvantages of behaviors before judging. While that assertive behavior you experience from someone may be difficult sometimes, that same behavior also drives action and gets things done. Remember, there is no good or bad, nor right or wrong, but there is effective or ineffective.

Motivators

▶ Review the assessments for key insights and takeaways.

- Examine the graphs for dimension scores, discussing importance in each dimension and how that connects to behavior and decisions.

- Examine the graphs for dimension rankings, discussing impacts in each dimension and how that drives behavior and decisions.

- Explore the differences in individual scores compared to the general population and how those differences may be expressed.

- Examine how the combination of Motivators create synergy or tension.

- Read personalized statement sets detailing how each dimension is defined by the score. Look for patterns by exploring the combination of the dimensions.

- Review the Word Matrix and look for patterns or tensions in the descriptors, comparing each dimension.

▶ Have conversations. Don't make assumptions; ask questions.

- When interacting with others, be careful not to put them in a Motivator box. All high styles do not act the same. Instead, discuss the ways those scores impact their core values and beliefs.

- Ask others about their experiences in various environments, situations, or relationships to understand more about how the individual Motivator shows up for them. Pay attention to the key circumstances that may impact effectiveness or satisfaction of the Motivator drivers.

▶ Discuss how the combination of Motivators creates synergy or tension and how that aligns (or doesn't) with behavior and emotions.

- Look through the lens of simple, practical, and applicable by asking questions to get to the root of why the Motivator is so important: What am I personally doing that supports satisfying this Motivator? Are there things I may need to do differently to be sure I am living in alignment (behaviorally) with my Motivators?

▶ Find opportunities for practice and application.

- Use all conversations to practice identifying the Motivators of others using observable descriptors and listening for core value patterns.

- Be authentically open and curious to learn about others' drivers, particularly when they are not like yours.

- Consider advantages and disadvantages of different motivational patterns before judging. While that high Regulatory Motivator you experience from someone may be difficult sometimes, that same thing also can be very helpful in getting things done right. Remember, there is no good or bad, nor right or wrong—but there is effective or ineffective. Be open to what others might value that is different than what you do.

An Intro To Thinking Styles: Critical Thinking (Hartman Value Profile)

W hile creating a solid understanding of human behavior and emotion through DISC provides a partial foundation of self-awareness, just like the layers of an onion, understanding what people are all about goes deeper than that.

As we've shared previously, we know that the most successful people share a common trait of self-awareness. Another element that brings a deeper understanding and clearer insight into who we are and why we do what we do is our Critical Thinking style. By building a comprehensive knowledge of our own thinking patterns, natural processing mechanisms, and biases (both positive and negative), we can begin to determine how to effectively maximize our critical thinking and decision-making capabilities.

Then, through building a greater understanding of the ways in which thinking happens in general, it becomes easier to see how these patterns influence and guide others' critical thinking and decision-making as well. Just like understanding the values, behaviors, and emotions of those around us, if we knew more about how people think and could better grasp how they process and what their biases are, how might we be able to better leverage strengths, regulate limitations, and seek balanced judgment as individuals and with others?

Understanding The Critical Thinking (Hartman Value Profile) Assessment

Better judgment means better decisions. Our decisions precede our actions, and actions precede results; our results are influenced by the critical thinking and decision-making skills we harness and apply.

Thankfully, thinking and mental processing ability, like musical talent or sports talent, can be learned and improved. But improving our thinking can require a great deal of time, effort, energy, and practice. What's more, even training is not a guarantee of success in making better decisions. Knowing something and applying it are two different things.

Understanding our judgment ability and how we process information is an essential benchmark to our ability to become more effective critical thinkers and processors. When we understand our thinking patterns and biases, we can take action to overcome the potential limitations they may create, and be sure we are actively and intentionally examining our decision-making in a way that brings balanced judgment and clarity.

The Critical Thinking assessment and report documents our natural selection process when we make decisions. It reflects how we take in information, process it, create a plan to act on it, and then follow through on that plan. It reveals our unique judgment patterns, biases, and filters that will affect our critical thinking skills and ultimate outcomes.

Keep in mind, there are many other things that can affect critical thinking as well, including behavioral style, emotional intelligence, reasoning ability, and blind spots. Furthermore, some thinking talents can be a great asset in some situations, but may become a hindrance in other circumstances.

Measuring Critical Thinking

In the late 1950s, Robert S. Hartman began work to measure judgment in an objective and accurate way, work that was then furthered after thirty-five years of nonstop validation by Wayne Carpenter. It was Carpenter who put into place the first computerized analysis using the terms that are still the foundation of measuring critical thinking today: *Empathy, Practical Judgment, Systems Judgment, Self-Esteem, Role Awareness, Self-Direction,* and interpretation through *Clarity* and *Attention*.

Using these measures, the Critical Thinking assessment provides insight into the capacity to make sound, balanced judgments about the world and in regard to themselves. It is imperative that we remember this is not a traditional self-assessment tool. It is a forced ranking assessment that objectively examines how people think and focuses specifically on thinking patterns that happen naturally and subconsciously. In essence, it measures what people's brains choose, before they even know what they're choosing!

The Science Behind The Report

Our judgment is comprised of both *World* (external) and *Self* (internal) scores in three dimensions: Intuitive Thinking, Practical Thinking, and Systems/Conceptual Thinking.

World scores evaluate *Empathy* (how well we understand other people and what they feel), *Practical Judgment* (how well we understand the results and what needs to be done to reach them), and *Systems/Conceptual Judgment* (how well we understand how things need to be done, with awareness of constraints, rules, and structured approaches).

Self scores evaluate *Self-Esteem* (how well we understand ourselves and how much value we assign to ourselves), *Role Awareness* (how well we understand our roles and how much importance we place on what we do), and *Self-Direction/Future View* (how well we understand our vision and plan for the future and how important the future is to us).

While each of these dimensions is measured separately in the assessment, the World Dimensions are affected by the Self Dimensions; essentially, how we think and feel about ourselves can have an impact on what we think and how we interact with the world around us. For example, if my self-esteem is low, I may not take risks to get what I want. Just like DISC and Motivators styles, our Thinking styles are related to one another as well.

Once we understand the categories that are measured, it is necessary to understand how they are measured. Thinking styles are measured with two scales: *Clarity* and *Attention*.

Clarity

Clarity is a measure of our natural ability to see and understand each dimension. The greater our clarity, the more accuracy and precision we have in judgments made in that dimension. Clarity is measured as:

- **Crystal Clear:** The ability to be very insightful, to distinguish differences, and to be sensitive to all aspects of the dimension.

- **Clear:** The ability to be in touch with key aspects of the dimension, but to overlook some aspects due to allowing some information in and filtering other information out.

- **Unconventional******:** Represents out-of-the-box thinking or mindset, indicating a natural ability to see things and respond to them in ways others overlook due to the ability to think differently than others.

- **Visible:** The ability to be in touch with and distinguish some specific aspects of a dimension clearly, but a strong tendency to overlook or not see other aspects due to selective filtering.

- **Transition:** Indicates the value dimension is unclear and likely to result in inaccurate or inconsistent decision-making, leading to mistakes in judgment.

**While it only applies to the World Dimension, Unconventional is the same level of clarity as Clear. It is the ability to be in touch with some key aspects but overlook others, all while having an unusual and unique perspective that is often unlike the perspective of others.

Attention

Attention is a measure of our natural ability to filter data and information to make a decision or how much importance we place on that dimension. Attentiveness or inattentiveness can be a strength or a limitation depending on the demands of the environment and the degree of balance with the other dimensions. Attention is measured as:

- **Overattentive:** Having a bias toward the dimension and a tendency to place a great deal of importance on it.

- **Attentive:** Having a balanced and generally positive view of the dimension and the ability to pay attention to it without losing perspective of other dimensions.

- **Cautious:** Exhibiting caution and skepticism regarding the dimension's importance. Tending not to focus or rely on it to make decisions.

- **Inattentive:** Filtering out the dimension, not seeing the importance of it. Tending to be skeptical or critical and undervaluing it. (Note: good clarity may reduce some effects of inattentiveness.)

There is a sweet spot in these two measures. The combination that leads to the greatest opportunity for sound, balanced judgment is *Crystal Clear* and *Attentive*. With excellent understanding and a balanced level of importance, the best, most balanced decisions can be made intentionally.

Bringing Together Clarity And Attention

Using the following table, you can see how each of the six areas brings together clarity and attention, defining not only how well you understand each dimension, but also how you value it.

Core Dimensions	World Dimensions	Self Dimensions
PEOPLE Intuitive Thinking	Empathy Measures how clearly you understand the impact your decisions will have on others, and the importance you place on how others feel about your decisions and actions.	Self-Esteem Measures how clearly you see your own value, strengths and limitations, and how much value you place on your own worth and appreciation of self.
TASKS Practical Thinking	Practical Judgment Measures how clearly you understand the best approach and the consequences of your decisions/actions to reach a specific result, and the importance you place on what's practical to reach those results.	Role Awareness Measures how clearly you see and understand your personal/social and professional roles, contributions, and functionality, and the importance you place on how those roles are relevant and fulfilling.
SYSTEMS Conceptual Thinking	Systems Judgment Measures how clearly you understand and appreciate systems, order, and structured thinking for planning and organizing things effectively, and the importance you place on protocols, guidelines, and constraints.	Self-Direction/Future View Measures how clear your vision of your future is and your confidence in what it entails, and the importance you place on reaching that destination as you have imagined it will be.

Critical Thinking Report Results

Using the Hartman Value Profile model, the Critical Thinking report was designed to be a simple and practical way to make that science user-friendly and immediately applicable. The report provides a combined score of your Clarity and Attention in each of the six dimensions, and a personal statement and explanation of how that dimension likely shows up in your own thinking and processing. In addition, you'll receive a bulleted list of your personal skills and capabilities in each area, as well as suggestions for awareness of risks and potential improvement to help you leverage your skills as effectively as possible in each dimension.

Furthermore, the report results will outline your own evaluation of where you place the greatest importance in comparing the World versus Self views to one another to see in which you place a higher value. Then, through comparison of the three dimensions in each, you'll see how you value People, Tasks, and Systems within each of those perspectives.

Benefits Of Understanding Critical Thinking

There are a number of benefits of understanding our critical thinking capacity for individuals and organizations. Not only is our self-awareness broadened, but this insight allows us to become even more adept at making the right, balanced decisions intentionally. If we understand our own Thinking style patterns and biases, we can purposefully ensure we are considering everything we should prior to making a decision and not making judgments based on our own, potentially limited, perspectives.

As we embrace intentional critical thinking and decision-making, we can also bring greater awareness to our understanding of the Thinking styles of others. It may take energy and commitment to make informed, impartial, and objective decisions, but it can be done effectively in a way that positively affects our results.

One of the most useful ways Critical Thinking can be applied is in bringing awareness to the thinking style, strengths, and potential risks when used in combination with DISC and Motivators for hiring and selection. By evaluating this trifecta of results, you can identify important patterns and key insights into what will help or hinder one's ability to find success, satisfaction, and effectiveness as well as how to support and develop them within the organization in a way that is proven to work.

An Intro To Emotional IQ Styles: Emotional Intelligence (EIQ)

Emotional Intelligence (EIQ) is a way of recognizing, understanding, and choosing how we think, feel, and act. It shapes our understanding of ourselves (intrapersonal) and our interactions with others (interpersonal). Intrapersonal recognition and management deals with recognizing, acknowledging, and working with our own emotions and expression. Interpersonal recognition and management examines relationships, empathy, connection, and social skills. EIQ is all about exploring how we perceive, access, generate, understand, express, and regulate our emotions and the emotions of others in ways that work to further our effectiveness and connections, rather than undermine them.

EIQ continues to be an increasingly hot topic in business and personal development. It also is a fairly controversial topic with two main schools of thought:

- EIQ is essential to personal and professional effectiveness.

- EIQ is soft, sensitive, unnecessary, even distracting, and should be left outside of the workplace.

Fortunately, more now than ever before, the former perspective is taking precedence over the latter: EIQ is essential to effectiveness.

The importance of EIQ can easily be measured in personal and professional success in many areas, including:

- Communication
- Decision-making
- Leadership
- Sales
- Teamwork and Team Performance
- Productivity
- Relationship Satisfaction
- Customer Service
- Conflict Management
- Overall Effectiveness

Research shows high levels of EIQ result in improved decision-making, decreased occupational stress, reduced staff turnover, increased personal well-being, increased leadership ability, and increased team performance. Bottom line: it matters.

Understanding The Emotional Intelligence Assessment

The EIQ assessment report provides insight into our own perceptions of our EIQ. Since it is a self-assessment, we only see our own thoughts about our level of skill and capability in EIQ unless we complete a 360-degree version to invite other perceptions. While this self-perspective may be limited initially, the information is still incredibly useful in building awareness of the elements measured in the assessment.

Each of the areas measured is developed with significant information on scores, details of what the scores represent, comprehensive information about how the subcategories impact the overall scores, personalized statement sets that highlight each area, and suggestions for improvement with reflection activities to create an action plan.

Measuring Emotional Intelligence

Unlike other assessments that have no right or wrong answers, and where the scores are not necessarily associated with a positive or negative connotation, EIQ is an assessment where the higher the score, the better the result. That said, even the highest score possible, 100 percent, is not indicative of perfection. EIQ is a constantly evolving, living, and breathing entity, so even an incredibly high score does not mean someone has mastered EIQ. A 100 percent simply represents that in the moment the assessment was completed, the individual had a solid grasp on that particular area. Just like DISC, though, our EIQ can shift at any time.

Consider this example of a client who recently went through a difficult and highly emotional divorce. June completed her assessment before the divorce was even a consideration; her scores in EIQ were quite high in every category. She was definitely a person who recognized and managed her emotions effectively, most of the time. However, on the morning after she moved out of her home and filed for divorce, June felt numb, strangely sensitive, disconnected, tired, and withdrawn yet craving interaction with those who loved her. In an instant, her entire world had changed. While a few months before, she was high in her EIQ, in this new phase of her life, June felt unprepared, unsure of who she was today and who she would become tomorrow as a divorced, single mother.

While her capacity to understand how EIQ works had not changed, she clearly was in a different space of creating a new understanding of *her own* emotional intelligence. Her high scores may have changed to something drastically lower during that transition time as she sought to find her footing in her new circumstances, facing new emotions.

Was June still capable of high EIQ? Absolutely. But her present circumstances created a shift in her ability to recognize and manage her emotions in those moments in the ways she was accustomed to before. And, her attention to her own EIQ changed. She had to reconnect with her emotions to get back to 100 percent in recognition and management for herself and in her relationships—and that took some time.

EIQ is measured through two competencies—*Recognition* and *Management*—with two perspectives—the *Self* and *Social*—resulting in four quotients. The assessment focuses on the ability to recognize, understand, and manage our own emotions (intrapersonal communication/self), and the ability to recognize, empathize, and relate to others (interpersonal communication/social). Within each area, an overall score is provided. That score is also dependent on our capability or skill in each area and attention to it. Sometimes a score will be low, not because we don't understand or know what to do, but because there is a lack of attention being given to that area at that time. It is important to discuss and determine if a lower score is from a challenge in capability or skill, or a lack of focus and attention in that area.

	Self *Intrapersonal*	Social *Interpersonal*
Recognition	**Self-Recognition** • Self-confidence • Awareness of emotions • Recognizing cause and effect in emotion • Paying attention to changes in emotional states	**Social Recognition** • Empathy • Picking up the moods of others • Caring what others are going through • Reading both verbal and nonverbal signals
Management	**Self-Management** • Creating goals and direction • Discipline and self-control • Upholding personal standards • Flexibility and adaptability • Optimism • Motivation and Initiative	**Social Management** • Sustaining quality relationships • Handling conflict effectively • Leadership and influence • Collaboration, cooperation, and teamwork • Effective interaction

Four Quotients And Twenty Subcategories

To further develop EIQ understanding, each of the four quotients is then divided into five measured subcategories that relate to the whole and provide a much more detailed perspective on how our EIQ is effected in that particular quotient. For each subcategory, we also receive a score and personalized information about that score. The quotients and subcategories are as follows:

Self-Recognition includes things like mental attitude, comfort and discomfort, strengths and weaknesses, biofeedback, self-acceptance, self-esteem, temperament, tension and stress levels, spirituality and conscience.

- **Self-Awareness/Understanding:** a conscious, deliberate reflection on personal identity, image, feelings, motivations, desires, and how these are associated with perceptions of self in the context of various situations. Empathy and understanding of self. Knowing why emotions occur.

- **Connections of Cause and Effect:** recognition of the impact and consequence of behaviors on feelings and moods; separating external and internal factors affecting emotions. Knowing how feelings relate to performance.

- **Self-Appreciation, Acceptance, and Confidence:** development of self-esteem, personal worth, and value; accepting and leveraging personal attributes. Recognizing personal strengths, weaknesses, and limitations. Operating with realistic self-assurance.

- **Consciousness and Assertiveness:** intentional establishment of personal boundaries and appropriate limits; choosing a path that expresses self-worth through personal care and outward presence.

- **Emotional Identification:** ability to identify and name personal feelings; vocabulary and definition of emotions allowing choices of expression, responses, and performance; effective reflection on intrapersonal information.

Social Recognition includes empathy, understanding/compassion, sensitivity/thoughtfulness, appreciation, holistic communication, rapport, connection, and understanding relationships.

- **Empathy, Sensitivity, and Appreciation:** understanding others; accurately picking up emotional cues from communication (including words, tone, and nonverbal signals); managing direct and indirect feedback effectively; being attentive, sensitive, aware, and appreciative of the emotional signals of others.

- **Service, Compassion, and Benevolence:** operating with a sense of contribution; aiding, helping, coaching, and developing others; giving; operating constructively to contribute to the emotional states and benefits of others; recognizing needs, wants, and desires; relating to alternative thoughts, perceptions, and perspectives.

- **Holistic Communication:** the ability to effectively send and receive information including emotional content; listening; engaging and connecting with others; sending and receiving verbal and nonverbal signals constructively.

- **Situational Perceptual Awareness:** recognizing and processing dynamic, shifting emotional data; communicating attention, focus, awareness, and connection; adapting to situational variables and changes; understanding which factors count and how much, and responding with reasonable behavior.

- **Interpersonal Development:** growing and nurturing constructive connections; setting the tone for long-term depth and breadth in relationships; focusing on quality in personal and professional relations; building resonance and rapport.

Self-Management includes restraint, discipline, control, resolve, direction/purpose, emotional management, flexibility, enthusiasm/excitement.

- **Self-Control and Discipline:** effectively handling impulses; maintaining composure while experiencing stressful, trying emotions; managing preparation and performance; actively and intentionally making choices; self-directing; emotionally persisting to achieve strategic objectives.

- **Goal-Directed Performance and Targeted Action:** focus to achieve long-term desired goals; emotional tenacity and persistence; drive to choose challenging objectives and assume acceptable risk; staying the course to completion; resilience in the face of obstacles and setbacks; seizing opportunities.

- **Integrity and Trustworthiness:** the ability to work with conscience, ethics, and integrity; operating with personal standards, principles, and values; being dependable, reliable, and authentic; keeping promises and assuming personal responsibility.

- **Motivation, Positive Psychology, and Initiative:** self-energizing; the ability to be mentally and emotionally engaged; attitude; passion; being responsible for personal success; acting and choosing feelings in accordance with positive emotions, optimism, and constructive feelings; limiting negative emotions, patterns, and spirals.

- **Creativity, Agility, Flexibility, and Adaptability:** coping with change, transition, and development; adjusting to situations, relationships, and feelings; handling curiosity and imagination to create, discover, and explore opportunities; innovation for progress; cognitive and emotional shifts to augment and manage change; the ability to problem solve and think outside the box.

Social Management includes directing, encouragement, building friendships, supporting, social poise, warmth, team results, collaboration.

- **Developing Relationships and Getting Along with Others:** cultivating, nurturing, and maintaining long-term personal and professional relationships; having quality connections and friendships.

- **Leadership and Influence:** operating with warmth, likability, presence, charisma, and approachability; paying attention and focusing on results; being involved, engaging, passionate, and powerful; showing deliberate persuasion; delivering solutions and success to others and to groups; partnering for targeted outcomes.

- **Change Catalyst and Response:** recognizing the need for change and championing action; developing interpersonal skills and abilities; initiating growth and progress on individual, team, and organizational levels. Focusing on positive outcomes.

- **Negotiation and Conflict Management:** bargains with abundance thinking for mutual gains; copes with conflict through positive proactive and reactive techniques; effectively deals with difficult people and situations; creates unity, balance, and gain.

- **Teamwork and Collaboration:** builds bonds; transforms groups into teams; fosters unified, engaged effort; generates collaboration, cooperation, participation, and high-quality results; nurtures the ability to develop synergy.

With Other Assessments In Mind

Using EIQ in combination with other assessments can bring powerful insight that may not be as clearly understood if the assessments are used independently. Looking at a combination of DISC and EIQ, for example, we can see how a person with the same behavioral style may express and respond to emotions differently, depending on their EIQ. A high Dominant style with high EIQ is likely to be perceived as ambitious, driving, decisive, and assertive. A high Dominant style with low EIQ is likely to be perceived as aggressive, demanding, bossy, and confrontational. The combination is one key to understanding why the same behaviors are expressed differently.

Examining EIQ alone is not always enough to reveal greater insight, but using a variety of tools allows a deeper look at how the whole person is impacted by measures in more than one focus area.

Benefits

There are a number of benefits of understanding EIQ for individuals and organizations. Our self-awareness blossoms with each new collection of information, and this insight gives us the opportunities to see how we connect with and express our own emotions and how we navigate effectively and appropriately the emotions of others to build stronger relationships. Having mutually beneficial, mutually respectful, and connected relationships is required to reach personal and professional effectiveness, and EIQ is a foundational viewpoint to navigate those interactions with expertise.

CHAPTER 9

In Closing

Before you picked up this book, you probably already knew predicting human behavior is not a simple proposition. After reading it, we hope you have a more educated opinion about how assessments can help you understand what makes humans tick. It is a process that is both a science and an art.

We started by acknowledging that people prediction is risky business, and brought up some of its critics' valid concerns. It's true that many assessments and tools are available, and their quality varies. Organizations can use the wrong thing in the wrong situations, and not all assessments are created equal. Chapter 1 provided plenty more food for thought, including the problems created because the assessment industry is unregulated.

These issues provided a backdrop for our quest to find instruments that would boost professional performance beyond anything previously available within the people analysis field—by exploring the whole person.

When used in business, quality assessments are flexible and capable of embracing optimization for a complete professional spectrum: customer service, vocational, technical, sales, management, or executive needs. It's important for employees to have the necessary skills to demonstrate the attitudes and behaviors that will enable them to succeed within each company's unique environment. When used in personal and professional relationships, great assessments reveal perceptions and perspectives that can either hinder or enhance our ability to connect, communicate, and interact in a way that supports mutual growth and understanding.

Why Should Assessments Be Used?

Here are nine proven reasons assessments are valuable:

1. **Improve Hiring and Selection.** The right person in the right job is vital. A bad hire is not only costly, but also can be detrimental to an organization. Using assessments, strengths and potential risks of job applicants can be identified *before* the interview and thoughtful, scientifically informed decisions can be made.

2. **Increase Sales.** Sales teams can be taught powerful behavior observation skills that work, and apply them in an effective sales cycle. Assessments can help them to see their own sales strengths and development areas, and focus on going from good to great in their interactions with others.

3. **Create World-class Leaders.** Building a leadership team of forward-thinking, engaging, supportive, and effective leaders isn't always easy. Ensuring they continue to be the best leaders they can be for their teams requires constant awareness and continued focus on honing their skills.

4. **Increase Productivity.** Measure performance and identify crucial companywide issues. Identify, with scientific accuracy, the gaps across an organization's key performance areas: culture, operations, leadership, training, service.

5. **Reduce Employee Turnover.** Ensure employees' needs and wants are met in a way that increases employee satisfaction, happiness,

and engagement, and helps them feel like what they're doing makes a difference in a way they value.

6. **Create Connected Teams.** Build effective, connected teams in an environment of coachability and transparency by embracing how behavior, motivation, thinking, and emotional expression impact interpersonal relationships and business success.

7. **Model Team Building.** Know which styles are going to work best together and what potential conflicts may arise. Build diverse teams based on compatible skills, traits, and styles for maximum efficiency and improved culture.

8. **Make the Right, Bright Decisions.** Critical thinking and decision-making are vital success skills. In day-to-day decisions or strategic plans, identifying what risks may exist is essential in building a strong organization capable of innovation and responding effectively to change.

9. **Customize Employee Training.** Discover how people communicate and tailor training toward their learning. Target styles to make training more effective and "sticky" the first time, reducing costly retraining efforts and lost productivity.

Chapter 2 explained clearly one view is not enough to accomplish all this, but by using assessments in combination, the ability to achieve the benefits listed above is improved.

Which Assessments Are Available?

We shared that our research has identified specific assessments to help identify and explore behavior styles, motivational styles, thinking styles, and emotional intelligence.

Our goal was to provide a deeper dive to understand the nuances of these assessments, examine how they accomplish what they do, and provide illustrative case histories of them in action. Along the way, we discussed topics such as strengths and challenges, as well as needs, fears, and emotions, expressed versus concealed behaviors, and natural and adapted styles.

Starting with DISC, we pointed out that this assessment is not a measure of intelligence, skills, education, experience, or an indicator of values. Rather, it identifies how behavioral patterns influence what a person wants, needs, and expects from you and others, and how people communicate those wants, needs, and expectations. Adding Motivators as a part of the equation provides a deeper look at why we do what we do by revealing another layer of what makes us tick and applying that to our own self-understanding and relationships with others. DISC and Motivators are a powerful combination.

For both DISC and Motivators, we provided their benefits to individuals and organizations, as well as common challenges and concerns of each assessment.

We also introduced a Thinking styles assessment: Critical Thinking (Hartman Value Profile). By building a comprehensive knowledge of our own thinking patterns, natural processing mechanisms, and biases (positive and negative), we can begin to determine how to effectively maximize our critical thinking and decision-making capabilities. Then, through building a greater understanding of the ways in which thinking happens in general, it becomes easier to see how these patterns influence and guide others' critical thinking and decision-making as well.

The Emotional Intelligence (EIQ) assessment was presented as well. EIQ is all about exploring how we perceive, access, generate, understand, express, and regulate our emotions in ways that work to further our effectiveness and connections with others, rather than undermine them. By using EIQ in combination with other assessments, we are able to bring greater awareness to our emotions and our expression, and better understanding of the emotions of others.

Assessments 24x7 specializes in assessment technology, and offers other assessment solutions that are not shared in this book. You are encouraged to explore what other solutions might support you and your clients.

Assessments In Action And Checklists

We included case study examples featuring the use of DISC and Motivators, along with observations and insights made along the way and successful strategies with the hope that it's relatable and clearly demonstrates the value that can be achieved by correctly using assessments. We also provided a checklist for applying the DISC and Motivators assessments.

The case studies reflect something we noted at the beginning of the book: while each of the assessments measures something vastly important to the whole person equation, it is the combination that brings the real power of understanding. Everyone has a different story, and the goal is that these assessments and the information they offer allow us to learn more about ourselves and others to be as effective and intentional as possible. With that in mind, we sincerely hope you're looking forward to learning more and continuing to grow your knowledge and skills.

APPENDIX

Acknowledgements

This book is due to a combination of incredible minds who contributed content either directly or indirectly and shaped the way this information came together. We are so honored and grateful for each of you who contributed to the success of the authors and the journey of this book to publication.

To those who shared their valuable knowledge to make this possible, we thank you very much: Dr. Russ Watson, Steven Sisler, Zeke Lopez, Robert Jerus, Dr. Jon Warner, Greg Smith, Pamela Brooks, Michael Bouton, Curt Engelmann, Mark Snow, Greg & Bob Carkhuff, Dr. Dennis Koerner, Jane Roqueplot, Dr. Michael O'Connor, Steve Healy, Mike Esterday, Merrick Rosenberg, and Cathy Hanson.

We wish to thank those who have paved the way for this work with their research and writings, as well as their commitment to this industry: Katherine Briggs, Jim Cathcart, John Geier, Phil Hunsaker, Carl Jung, Florence Littauer, William Marston, David McClelland, David Merrill, Isabel Briggs Myers, and Larry Wilson.

We gratefully acknowledge Henry DeVries of Indie Books International, without whom this book would still be just an idea. We also give endless thanks to those who provided valuable feedback and support through this process, especially: Laura Bruno, Bonnie Burn, Susan Cranston, Sandra Davis, Lynnette Embree, Brinna Gard, Kyle Gillette, Eric Grossberger, Sue Koch, Amy Lewis, Ulrik Lork, Greg Phillips, Kevin McCarthy, Barbara & Rich Meiss, Jaymini Mistry, Ira Tau, and Roel Schaart.

This book would not exist without the combined efforts of our extraordinary writing team. We'd like to acknowledge the significant involvement of one author in particular, Jennifer Larsen. While including insights from the team, Jennifer invested countless hours bringing this book to fruition, from capturing her knowledge and expertise through years of work with others, to diligently writing and sharing it all in a simple, practical, and accessible format. Her remarkable contributions—to this book, to our community, to the industry, and mostly to the Assessments 24x7 team—are incredibly valued and appreciated.

Finally, we owe a great debt of appreciation to each of you—our friends, family, clients, partners, and curious learners—who take the time to read, ask, apply, and continue to desire to make a difference with this work. It is with you in mind that we do all we do.

About Assessments 24x7

Assessments 24x7 was founded by Dr. Tony Alessandra and Brandon Parker. Separated by thirty years of life experience, the New Yorker got paired up with the California kid. This unlikely match was the result of a wrong turn, a random airline flight, sitting next to the right person, the confidence of a twenty-two-year-old junior programmer, and Alessandra's intuition to trust. Alessandra had a vision and Parker had the technical skills. That was the recipe for the beginning days of Assessments 24x7 over two decades ago. Assessments 24x7 has partnered with companies large and small, coaches, consultants, and trainers to give them tools to succeed. Leading organizations and coaches use Assessments 24x7's assessment technology to guide their strategy for hiring and selection, performance evaluations, skills training, team building, conflict management, promotion and succession planning, organizational restructuring, employee retention, and leadership development.

As a Global Leader in Assessment Technology, Assessments 24x7 has over twenty years of expertise in this business. With more than twenty-five different assessment offerings, certification programs, training materials, and more, the company has supported the use of over 7 million assessments in behavior, motivation, emotional intelligence, and critical thinking. The company has grown to include a powerful team of marketing specialists, design professionals and IT experts, a world-class training and instructional design department, an outstanding customer care group, and a winning sales team.

About The Authors

Brandon Parker

Brandon Parker has pioneered numerous custom website projects, from basic design and marketing to comprehensive data-driven programs. In 2000, he partnered with Dr. Tony Alessandra to build, from the ground up, the software systems used today by Assessments 24x7's global assessment community. With his hands involved since day one, there is no one more familiar with the technical and user components of the assessment software. From the beginning, Parker has been instrumental in developing and growing Alessandra's vision for the company, and is involved with a very hands-on approach to actively manage day-to-day operations.

As CEO of Assessments 24x7, Parker is proud to have an incredible team that works extremely hard. He is never too busy to provide world-class service by discussing strategy, supporting client efforts, and answering assessment-related questions. Parker is known in the industry as the go-to guy for helping businesses achieve their assessment goals.

Parker earned his BA from Chapman University in Orange, California. In his free time, Brandon enjoys spending time with his wife, daughter, and pets. He prefers the mountains to the city, and looks forward to having as much time outside as possible. He enjoys boating, backpacking, fishing, and hiking.

Jennifer Larsen, MAEd, MSP, MBA

Jennifer Larsen is Assessments 24x7's VP of Instructional Design and Certification. She also serves as coach and mentor, professional values analyst, and instructional designer for client customization and resource development. She specializes in helping clients, coaches, and facilitators understand unique assessment results, and assists individuals and groups in personal and professional development.

Through educating others in improving communication, understanding critical thinking, evaluating emotional intelligence, and aligning behavior and values, Jennifer seeks to infuse others with a passion for learning and growing, encourage self-awareness, and impart simple, practical, and applicable knowledge to help grow relationships and increase personal and professional effectiveness. Her career path has included individual and organizational development, secondary and adult education, customer service, corporate finance, and investor relations.

Larsen holds a Washington State Secondary Education Teaching Certificate, a BA in English with an emphasis in composition and rhetoric, an MA in adult education and training, an MS in psychology, and an MBA with an emphasis in human resource management. She is also certified in a variety of training courses and development workshops with many well-known vendors.

She has traveled all over the world, sharing her passion and expertise and training and certifying others to make a difference. She has delivered intimate and large-scale public and private presentations since 2001 to corporate, educational, and professional development audiences on topics such as leadership development, self-awareness and personal growth, relationships between men and women, building effective communication, and quality training programs. She is an avid painter, a professional singer, and stays very busy with her active family in Washington State.

Tony Alessandra, PhD

Tony Alessandra is founder and chairman of Assessments 24x7, a company that offers a variety of online assessments, including the widely used DISC profile, Motivators (Values/PIAV), Critical Thinking (Hartman Value Profile), Emotional Intelligence Quotient (EIQ-2), and several 360° effectiveness assessments.

As an author and speaker, Alessandra helps companies turn prospects into promoters. He is two speakers in one: a professor and a performer, or as one client put it—he delivers college-level lectures in a comedy store format. Alessandra offers audiences the opportunity to enjoy themselves while learning practical, immediately applicable skills that positively affect their relationships with prospects, customers, and coworkers. His focus is on how to create instant rapport with prospects, employees, and vendors; how to convert prospects and customers into business apostles who will "preach the gospel" about your company and products; and how to out-market, out-sell, and out-service the competition.

Alessandra has a streetwise, college-smart perspective on business, having been raised in the housing projects of NYC to eventually realizing success as a graduate professor of marketing, internet entrepreneur, business author, and hall-of-fame keynote speaker. He earned a BBA from Notre Dame, an MBA from the University of Connecticut, and a PhD in marketing from Georgia State University.

He is also a prolific author with thirty books translated into over fifty foreign language editions, including the newly revised, bestselling *The NEW Art of Managing People, Charisma, The Platinum Rule, Collaborative Selling*, and *Communicating at Work*.

He is featured in over one hundred audio/video programs and films, including DISC Relationship Strategies; The Dynamics of Effective Listening; and Gaining the EDGE in Competitive Selling. He is also the originator of the internationally recognized behavioral style assessment tool, The Platinum Rule.

Alessandra was inducted into the National Speakers Association (NSA) Speakers Hall of Fame in 1985. In 2009, he was inducted as one of the Veteran Speakers Retreat "Legends of the Speaking Profession;" from 2010 to 2014, he was selected five times as one of the Top 5 Sales/Marketing/Customer Service Speakers by Speakers.com. In 2010, he was elected into the inaugural class of the *Top Sales World* Sales Hall of Fame; in 2012, Global Gurus voted him one of the Top 50 Sales and Marketing Influencers; and in 2012, he was voted the #1 World's Top Communication Guru by Global Gurus.

Recognized by *Meetings & Conventions* magazine as "one of America's most electrifying speakers," his polished style, powerful message, and proven ability as a consummate business strategist consistently earn rave reviews and loyal clients.

Matthew Dickson

Matthew Dickson, former Chief Marketing Officer (CMO) of Assessments 24x7, joined the company in 2014. He is skilled at identifying, developing, and managing sales and marketing initiatives, including brand conceptualization and innovation, marketing and sales IP, marketing collateral development, website copywriting and layout, social media management, content marketing development, multimedia advertising management, email marketing creation, CS procedures and management, client consultations, and new account procurement. Dickson graduated magna cum laude with his BA in Journalism from San Francisco State University.

Before he began his career in sales and marketing, Dickson spent his first several professional years as the contributing writer and editor for more than a dozen magazines and alternative news weeklies. He was the youngest contributing editor in the twenty-plus-year history of *The Face* magazine (UK). His work was also widely published in New York's *Village Voice*, *The LA Weekly*, *The San Francisco Bay Guardian*, *Surface* magazine, *The Wire* magazine, *Black Book* magazine, and several others. At that time, Dickson